EARTH

Edited by Peter Carver

Peter Martin Associates Limited

Introduction

This collection of Canadian writing presents a kaleidoscope of voices from St. John's to Vancouver Island. Or, more accurately, from Andy Mouland's Musgrave Harbour to John Marshall's Seymour Inlet, from Bruce Cockburn's Highway 401 to Phillip Blake's Fort MacPherson.

Some are familiar voices, stars — W.O. Mitchell, Al Purdy, Matt Cohen, Roch Carrier, singers Gordon Lightfoot and Murray McLauchlan, newsman Harry Bruce, broadcaster Peter Gzowski. Others are not so well-known if only because they have not yet been heard by the national audience.

The theme is the land — Canada — and our varied ways of experiencing this often difficult, always absorbing country. Wrenching disappointments as well as triumphant highs; hardships and hopes.

Powerful voices. Depression survivors. Dene people. Denizens of the urban jungle. Pioneers. Loggers. Car-jockeys. Immigrants. Farmers, Urbanites. Accents from many levels of our society.

Their words bring that thrill of recognition which springs from a shared understanding of what it is to live here.

Their words should be read — and heard — aloud.

The language of *Earth* is sometimes tough, rigorous. It demands more than just casual attention. It arises from strong feelings generated by vivid experience. The kind of experience which can be just as enlarging and revealing as the more introspective moments in life. Each mood has its own language. Each is found in these pages.

In earthiness there is humour as well. In Al Purdy's rueful praise of Old Alex, Marc Plourde's hilarious account of classroom embarrassments, or Andy Macdonald's evocation of Cape Breton outhouse culture, there is that brand of humour one recognizes as a national characteristic. Two of the greatest delights are Newfoundlanders Ted Russell and Ray Guy — the latter the 1977 winner of the Leacock award for humour.

Earth provides a platform from which new voices can be heard. It reaffirms our enjoyment of more established figures. It reflects the vitality of our national experience, its diversity and essential unity. *Earth* celebrates the neighbourhood which is the nation.

Earth is the first of four volumes in the ELEMENTS series. The other titles are *Air, Fire* and *Water*.

Peter Carver

Contents

In the East Cornera the Pasture

"What's heaven like?" asked Art. "What's it like, Sammy?"

In a monotone, with the singsonging stress of a child's Christmas recitation, Saint Sammy began:

"To start with He give a flip to the fly-wheela thought, an' there was Heaven an' earth an' Him plumb in the middle. She had no shape ner nothin' on her. 'Let there be light,' He seth, an' there was some. 'Suits me fine,' He seth, 'an' I'm a-gonna call her night, an' I'm a-gonna call her day.' He took an' He gathered all the water together so the dry land stuck up; 'That there is dry earth,' He seth. 'Grass,' He seth, 'let her come.' An' she come. She jumped up green. He hung up the moon; he stuck up the sun; he pricked out the stars. He rigged out spring an' fall an' winter an' He done it. He made Him some fishes to use the sea fer swimmin' in—some fowls fer to use the air fer flyin' in.

"Next he made the critters.

"An' He got to thinkin', there ain't nobody fer to till this here soil, to one-way her, to drill her, ner to stook the crops, an' pitch the bundles, an' thrash her, when she's ripe fer thrashin', so He took Him some topsoil—made her into the shape of a man—breathed down into the nose with the breatha life.

"That was Adam. He was a man.

"He set him down ontuh a section to the east in the districka Eden—good land—lotsa water.

"The Lord stood back, an' He looked at what He done insidea one week an' she suited Him fine.

"He laid off fer a few days whilst Adam named over the critters. Then He remembered.

"He took Him onea Adam's ribs—whittled him a wife.

"That was Eve. She was a woman."

Steadily sibilant the wind washed through the dry grasses all around, bending them, laying them low, their millions yearning all together.

"You better git, boys," said Sammy. "Tarry not, fer the Lord's a-waitin' on me." His arm went up and around, pointing out his horses: great, black beasts with their tails blown along their flanks, their thick necks arched and pointing out of the wind. "He waits fer Sammy in the east cornera the pasture—the Lord's corner." Without another word he turned and took up his spry way in that direction.

from *Who Has Seen the Wind*, a novel by W.O. Mitchell

A Handful of Earth —to René Lévesque

Proposal:
let us join Quebec
if Quebec won't join us
I don't mind in the least
being governed from Quebec City
by Canadiens instead of Canadians
in fact the fleur-de-lis and maple leaf
in my bilingual guts
bloom incestuous

Listen:
you can hear soft wind blowing
among tall fir trees on Vancouver Island
it is the same wind we knew
whispering along Cote des Neiges
on the island of Montreal
when we were lovers and had no money
Once flying in a little Cessna 180
above that great spine of mountains
where a continent attempts the sky
I wondered who owns this land
and knew that no one does
for we are tenants only

Go back a little:
to hip-roofed houses on the Isle d''Orleans
and scattered along the road to Chicoutimi
the remaining few log houses in Ontario
sod huts of sunlit prairie places
dissolved in rain long since
the stones we laid atop of one another
a few of which still stand
those origins
in which children were born
in which we loved and hated
in which we built a place to stand on
and now must tear it down?

—and here I ask all the oldest questions
of myself
the reasons for being alive
the way to spend this gift and thank the giver
but there is no way

I think of the small dapper man
chain-smoking at PQ headquarters
Lévesque
on Avenue Christophe Colomb in Montreal
where we drank coffee together six years past
I say to him now: my place is here
whether Cote des Neiges Avenue Christophe Colomb
Yonge Street Toronto Halifax or Vancouver
this place is where I stand
where all my mistakes were made
when I grew awkwardly and knew what I was
and that is Canadian or Canadien
it doesn't matter which to me

Sod huts break the prairie skyline
then melt in rain
the hip-roofed houses of New France as well
but French no longer
nor are we any longer English
—limestone houses
lean-tos and sheds our fathers built
in which our mothers died
before the forests tumbled down
ghost habitations
only this handful of earth
for a time at least
I have no other place to go

Al Purdy

Slide Show

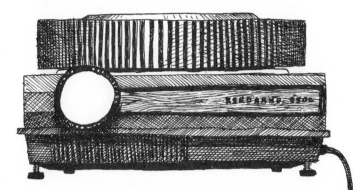

This picture that you see on that screen now is on New Year's Day. We were dancing in the community hall. The first couple you see is Abraham Francis and myself. The next couple is James Simon and Laura Thompson. And the next one was Fred Firth and Mrs. Blake, but they are behind, and we couldn't see Fred. This is what we call duck dance, and, boy, we enjoy ourselves there. . . .

This is in Aklavik in those days, across the river there, where they called it the Hudson Bay Channel. Eskimos used to land there and pitch up their tents, some houses there too, and you see the Eskimos those days with all of their big boats with big motor in it and they come up right after the ratting and some of them remain there for the summer. Look how nice Eskimos used to live too.

This is in Aklavik. This is the church and Austin's Cathedral used to be and this is how they used to go to the church. This is an ordination service, I think, but I don't really remember. And you could see Jim Edwards right there, Jim Sittichinli, Mr. Gibson—Reverend Gibson—and Bishop Marsh and Mr. Jones and Mr. Shepherd—you could just see his bald head there. . . .

This is in the same building, and they're still dancing.

And this is your old town, McPherson. All these buildings, the Indians, the men, build them for themselves. It is their own buildings and all done away with now and used to be so good. . . . There's their church and there is their community hall, that white building there, and this is what they

mean—that the Hudson's Bay got the highest spot in town. That's where they are way up there and they start moving us and moving us and finally they moved us into Marsh Lake way up there where it is swampy and dirty and so far for us to go to church. . . .

That is in the same community hall. This is in our community hall and the ones that are doing the jig, as you seen yesterday, people jig; it's Herbert Blake and that old lady is Harriet Stewart. They are dancing jig and you could see the people sitting around on the floor and the dance was on such a cold day, so they all have their parkas on, sitting on the floor watching. . . .

This is right down below from Hudson's Bay, right down below. There was a nice little creek running below here and you could see the hill is so different today and we used to land here right after the ratting. . . . Everybody packed their

belongings up on their back, nobody bothered about truck or anything to help them, we just packed everything up to our houses and we are still very, very happy doing that. Then soon the bulldozers came and they made the road on the side of that hill and now you can see the hill is not the same anymore.

And this is in the winter, our church. We have a fire in it whenever we are going to have church service. We have fire, wood; we're burning wood in this church and yet it is comfortable.

This is a day after Easter. We had a woman's auxiliary meeting in the mission house and after we came out we done so well and we were very, very happy with all our older people here, so we had the picture taken. This one standing first with pink parka on is Mrs. Elizabeth Kunizzi. She is still here. The next one is Mrs. Anne Blake, she is gone, and the next one is Louisa Snowshoe and in behind her that woman laughing and smiling so hard, that is Lucy Vaneltsi. And then in front, of course, is Harriet Stewart . . . so happy; she's laughing. Then behind her is Mrs. Edith Kay, she's still living, and then there is that one

smiling, showing her teeth, that is Sarah. . . .

Now, this is well known people. This old lady is still living, but the old man is gone. This is old Robert George and Mrs. Robert, and that little girl way behind there, that is Mary Kay. And this

9

Out along the prairie

is their own house which he built and they lived happily in there. The most happiest couple that I remember is these old people, and their daughters and their sons are sitting in here watching them. . . .

This old man, is Charlie Stewart when he is eighty-three—this is taken in 1956—and this is my daddy. He is the most happy man that ever lived. Lots of people remember him. This picture is right beside the mission house. Maybe the missionary gave him a cup of tea so he looks very happy. My father was a very good dancer. I think even now today, when they dance, like George Robert the other day told me that when he play the song for what we call duck dances, he remember him. That is the last dance he played for him and he was very light on his feet. That is why everybody remembers him dancing. I don't think that anybody is as light as my father. . . .

Sarah Simon from *The Past and Future Land*, by Martin O'Malley

---

We live in an empty place filled with wonders.

Peter Newman

Out along the prairie
Where the edges aren't hid,
They're painted there
Upon my eyelids.
Out along the prairie
Where the wind is so strong
I wonder what holds
The houses on.
And the land is so flat
And the lines are all straight
And the earth revolves
100,000 kph

Out along the prairie
In freefall I roll,
Into the sky
That empty blue hole.
Out along the prairie
With the hawk's wheel and spin
The edges keep changing
Where do they begin
And the land is so flat
And the lines are all straight
And the earth revolves
100,000 kph

Out along the prairie
Where cubists retire
When they've grown weary
Of Paris and her spires
Out along the prairie
Metaphor: the brain,
scrub-brush ganglia
Exposed to the rain
And the land is so flat
And the lines are all straight
And the earth revolves
100,000 kph

Joe Hall from his record, *impuls(e)* Vol.5, No. 2

Child's Song

Goodbye, Mama, goodbye to you too, Pa
Little sister, you'll have to wait a while to come along
Goodbye to this house and all its mem'ries
We all just got too old to say we're wrong
I've got to make one last trip to my bedroom
I guess I'll have to leave some stuff behind
It's funny who the same old crooked pictures
Just don't look the same to me tonight.

There ain't no use in shedding no more tears, Ma
And there ain't no use in shouting at me, Pa
I can't live no longer with your fears, Ma
I love you but that hasn't helped at all
All of us has gotta do what matters
And each of us must see what we can see
Though it was long ago you must remember
That you were once as young and scared as me.

Mama, I don't know how hard it is yet
When you realize you're growing old
I know how hard it is now to be younger
And I know you've tried to keep me from the cold
Thanks for all you've done - it may sound hollow
Thank you for the good times that we've known
But I must have my own road to follow
You will all be welcome in my home.

So I have got my suitcase, I must go now
I don't mind about the things you said
Sorry, Ma, I don't know where I'm going
And remember, little sister, look ahead
Tomorrow I'll be in some other sunrise
Maybe I'll have someone by my side
Mama, give your love back to your husband
Father, you have taught me well. Goodbye.

Goodbye, Mama, goodbye to you too, Pa.

                                    Murray McLauchlan

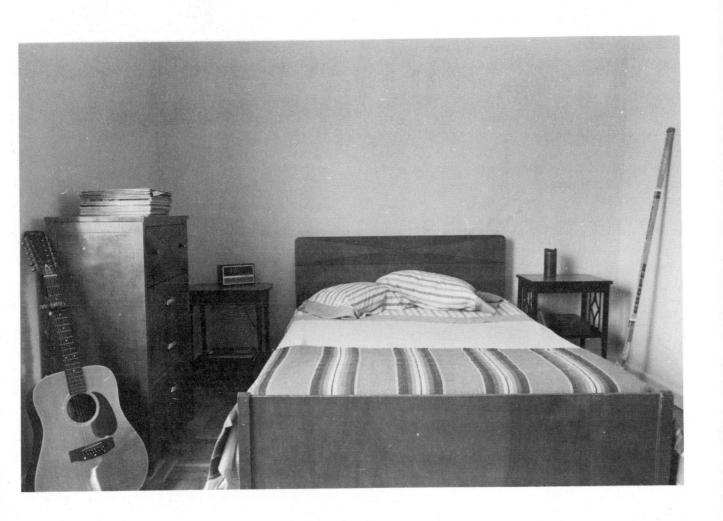

I Want to Get Out

At school I was loud, trying to get attention, craving it, my body getting out of proportion—narrow, stooped shoulders, wide hips and flabby—getting stupider as time went on. High school was worse—it was like prison. At sixteen after failing my first year in high school, I dropped out.

Life centred around poolrooms, gangs, street corners, mouthing off to people, being obnoxious and stealing.

Bugging people in petty ways, there was nothing else to do. No jobs. I didn't give a sweet damn about anyone or anything. Fancying myself a real tough guy, developing into a mouthy punk.

In the summer I worked sporadically at different fruit warehouses, as long as they would put up with me. When the trucks came in to be loaded for Toronto or Montreal, I used to beg the drivers to take me there and back with them. Toronto—Montreal—Detroit. I would really become alive and would work hard unloading their trucks, sleeping in the cab at night, freezing cold, hating the thought of going back home.

Different cities, markets, seeing the working people in the small hours of the morning, the hobos—and I knew I would never want to be part of that lonely scene.

The work, life centring around a bag of turnips. But I knew of no way out.

In an attempt to fight off the loneliness I lived in a part-time fantasy world where I would take my brother's 22 and my cap guns and pretend I was a pioneer in the woods and shoot just about everything in sight—trees, grapes, ducks, signs, frogs, crawfish.

The highlight of the year was the Heinz picnic or when the Conklin Shows carnival came to town. I used to hang around and wish I could go with them but I didn't. My conception of carnivals was far-out places of fun and no work. I was always a coward then, no matter what came to pass, progressing into a sneak thief—filching pennies, chocolate bars and any small items I could get my hands on.

I lived a double life—being the town asshole in the daytime and at home thinking it all over. Dear God, deliver me from this—there must be something else.

In the winter we stuck tar into trees that had worms. Orchards, branches, cold, a cigar from my father. I followed behind my father and brother, alone even at home. Take me with you!

Truck rides throughout the night. Detroit—Chicago—Cleveland—Toronto—Cincinn Wishing I could stay there. Playing Monopoly in someone's basement—the beginning of friendships that never lasted.

One July I sent an application to the army and got called to the London Barracks for my physical and mental.

Oh Shit Joy Hallelujah—it's really happening! I passed the medical. Then the great colossal bum trip. That night while I was asleep dreaming that a cat was pissing on me, I was black-balled, someone had rubbed shoe polish all over me. Half asleep and pissed off I took a shower for two hours trying to get it off. The next day I was called into the chief commander's office and was told they were rejecting me because of my school record and the bad reports of my teachers.

Defeat. Smashed to hell.

At this stage in my somewhat screwed-up life and mind I knew something was wrong, but I didn't know what. Working here and there, getting fired after a few days because of my mouth and my laziness. I had always been ashamed and blushing, stammering when I talked to people. It seemed like a mirage when I got into a conversation. The only way to get over it was to say what was on my mind—usually offensive.

All there seemed to be hanging around Leamington were the idiots who were raised there, and they got older, still not doing anything except driving around the main street twenty times on two wheels. Fifty morons crammed into a beat-up car trying to pick up girls with pimples on their faces.

Tomato patches—poolrooms—Heinz 57—gossiping, fucking idiots.

No man, I don't want to be part of this—I want to get out. Someday I will.

from *Annals of the Firebreather* by Marcel Horne

Randying

In these trying times let us once again turn for solace to that celebrated and inexhaustible volume "Guy's Encyclopedia of Juvenile Outharbour Delights." Let us idly turn the pages to the winter section.

Randying: One of the top Juvenile Outharbour Winter Delights, no doubt about it. A universal and vastly popular delight practiced from the first bit of ice on the bog holes in November to the last sketch of snow on the hill in April.

To go randying you have to have something to randy on. The list is long, but the most highly prized vehicle for randying on was the common coaster or youngster's sled as they say in the States. A versatile machine if ever there was one.

On a flat sheet of ice you held the coaster out in front of you, galloped along until you got up to takeoff speed, then flopped down on your stomach on the coaster until the momentum gave out.

The sprint-and-belly-flop method of taking off on a coaster was also useful on hills but only for the brave at heart if the hill was steep and icy.

On our favourite hill for randying you could easily break the sound barrier on a coaster if ice conditions were right. You also stood an excellent chance of breaking your neck in the fence at the bottom.

To make the necessary right-angle turn and avoid being meshed in the pickets you had to hold the steering gear right across her and drag your toes until your rubber boots started to smoke.

To qualify for the Legion of Honour in randying, however, you had to make this self-same death-dive lying flat on a coaster with two other riders stacked horizontally on your back.

On the eighty-nine degree slope to which I refer there was a nasty lump about halfway down. When a coaster struck this lump at about 900 miles an hour the two passengers were launched three feet up in the air to come down again on the back of the navigator with a sickening crunch. More bad backs were wrought by randying than this world dreams of.

A sideline of this type of randying was "Making Trains". With all hands lying flat on their coasters you made a train by hooking your toes into the bow of the coaster behind. You rattle down the hill in a long snake and there's the feeling of being caught up in the irresistible force of a buffalo stampede.

If one of the head coasters turned over he had the prospect of being run over by a dozen or more of those behind and being killed probably, if the hill was steep enough. Which is what made it so much fun.

There always came a time in an evening's randying when daredevilry reached and exceeded the bounds of sanity. This awesome moment came when some maniac suggested: "Let's go down sot up."

Now, anyone who has ever participated in the robust sport of randying knows that it is impossible to control a coaster sot up. The centre of gravity is raised, you see, and you can't dig in the toes of your rubber lumps to steer. Sheer lunacy.

To the best of my knowledge no one has ever gone down a respectable hill sot up on a coaster and crossed the finish line at the same time as the vehicle.

Suppose that two or three drunk with the smell of danger decided to go down on the same coaster sot up. Even before the halfway point was reached the air would be full of flying bodies and machinery. Even the more spectacular crashes at LeMans can't compare.

The icy grade would be littered with the bodies of the foolhardy, spinning round and round with great velocity toward the bottom. It has always surprised me that astronaut training doesn't include "going down sot up."

During lulls in the sport people lay quietly on their coasters at the bottom of the hill, vacant looks on their faces as the latest brush with death was savoured, idly kicking their feet to keep them warm, picking those little lumps of ice off their wool mitts, eating snow.

Suddenly one of the resting coaster buffs would let out a wild, unnatural, strangled yell. In the midst of a recuperative reverie someone had absentmindedly put his tongue on the frosty iron crossbar of his coaster and it had stuck fast. There's terror, pure and simple for you.

Oh, there were lots more things to randy on. Stave slides, hand slides, toboggans, pieces of cardboard and old floor canvas, book bags and pants seats.

When another winter closes about our aging heads, we'll look back for warmth on randying and other Juvenile Outharbour Winter Delights. It may help us survive.

from *That Far Greater Bay*, by Ray Guy

Work is what we have to do; play is what we like to do.

Hans Selye

First Thursday of the Month

It amazed me how missus Prudhomme could move so softly in her high heel shoes. She was a heavily built woman; not really fat, but tough. No one could hear her coming as she moved up from the rear, along the windowside of the room, stopping at the third desk of the second row. Her wooden ruler crashed down on the desk, less than an inch from the boy's fingers. At contact, the tip of it snapped and flew across the class. Missus Prudhomme's aim seldom faltered, yet, in the course of that school year she still managed to break several rulers, pointers, yard sticks and chalks. She grabbed the boy and the comic book and dragged him (he was the elder of the two Choquette brothers) by the hair to the front of the room, and made him kneel there below the crucifix on the wall. The comic book was of course torn to pieces and thrown in the waste paper basket—she resumed her patrol.

A lot of drama went into that last year at Saint Barthélémy Vimont grade school, 1963 it was, the year Pope John XXIII died and I had to write an essay about it. Missus Prudhomme, my teacher, liked religious subjects and I was scared shitless of her. I disguised myself in anonymity, doing as I was told, trying to be faceless among the sixty boys that made up our class 7B. I remember now very little about missus Prudhomme's teaching ability, only that she was the best enforcer and policeman, of a kind, in all Barthélémy Vimont. She originally came as a replacement for the lovely young non-disciplinarian Grade 3B teacher who (I've forgotten her name now) broke a leg during the Christmas vacations, trying out her new skis on Mount Royal. It seemed the nice ones always broke their legs, or had nervous breakdowns, or heart attacks, or just quit. Within less than a week of her arrival, missus Prudhomme gained renown. She was the only teacher who could, at any moment, demand total immediate silence and order from her class, and obtain it. When she said "Walk double file, in order of height!", it was done. She had a technique of slapping, where the back of the hand swerved at the last instant and it became a karate chop. The following year they promoted her to 7B.

The previous 7B teacher, a man, was going into retirement. He had been doing this for several years. One incident, though, prompted his decision: he slapped one of the older boys, one of his three-year-over flunkies (some as old as seventeen) and the boy gave back a quick jab, "just by reflex" he later said, which knocked the wind out of mister Como. Mister Como turned white and walked out of the room, doubled over, clutching his stomach—that was how the story went—and later they found the old guy downstairs, crying in the locker room.

Missus Prudhomme was keen on religion; we were all supposedly doing our monthly "examen de conscience" when she found Choquette with the comic book. It was not their first encounter. An "examen de conscience" was when you leaned forward and closed your eyes very tight, your head resting upon your arms criss-crossed over the desk; you were then thinking thoroughly and deeply about all the sins you had committed in the last month, retracing and categorizing each sinful action and thought. Even the wish to sin, someone told me, was itself sinful. Could I remember everything? Would I hide something? My head swirled round in theology and catechism till I saw stars, green, yellow, red, and the backs of my eyes hurt, and when I opened them, I felt sick and hot inside like I was already in hell.

This lasted about fifteen minutes. After, we would line up in rank along the door-side of the room, along the blackboard with the alphabet, white letters on black cards, trailing above it: A B C D . . . all the way to the rear of the room, all written in both capitals and small letters. I took my rank somewhere near Z, and they pushed me forward because I was not that tall. Our class with all the other classes from grade two upward, would then leave for Saint Roche's church, for mass and communion. The parish priest said a special 9.15 a.m. mass every first Friday for our school. The school system and the mother Church worked cooperatively in this way (and in a lot of other ways) to see that we were all kept in a state of grace, absolutely.

During the "examen de conscience" missus Prudhomme moved about the classroom, up and down the aisles. She had a set of prayer beads which she always kept in her purse. She took them out (they were very large, about three feet long) and she patrolled with them. Sometimes she would pray aloud, perhaps to inspire us as we probed our guilty consciences, "Je vous salue Marie, pleine de grace, le Seigneur est avec vous . . ." her fingers twitching along the ring of beads, till she found Choquette.

When I heard the noise, I lifted my head and it gave me a certain joy, seeing Choquette kneeling. I never liked him, especially since he played a trick on me once. Then I realised that feeling this pleasure was probably another sin which I would have to categorize and confess. I closed my eyes and again reviewed my list.

Anger: four times.

Pride: twice.

Disobeying figures of authority: five or six times.

Speaking evil of others: once a week, on the average.

Sex (in thought and action):————————————.

I hated confessing sex stuff and it was always hard for me to decide how many times this and how many times that, in this particular field. But if you withhold something in confession, especially a mortal sin (everything sexual was mortal), that also meant hell: eternal damnation, flames, devils with pitchforks, man-eating worms, infinite suffering. My face felt burning inside my palms; my fingers felt very cold crossing my forehead. I prayed, hoping for a vision, an angel of

God to come tell me everything was all right. This I never saw, but at times I pretended to myself that I did. Now my eyes hurt and again I saw stars, green, yellow, blue.

Choquette did not seem at all humiliated, kneeling at the front of the class. When missus Prudhomme turned, he also turned and snickered and made faces. Over the years, he, his brother, Tato and that big kid with the mustache, Labonté, appropriated the rear corner near the window. It was their policy that if they left the teacher alone, they should also be left alone. They were waiting to leave school and become rich working for the mafia, or they would do as one of their friends had done. He became a delivery boy for a grocery store on Saint Roche Street. During recess he would come by on his bicycle. He smoked huge cigars and gave away candies and gum to his old pals, to show off his success. The principal threatened to call the cops if he didn't get off the school grounds, because he was corrupting us, after all. The kid made a gesture, meaning "Go jack off".

Choquette and his gang hated school work, silence, lining up in ranks, and this new teacher. They threw pieces of eraser, paper clips and paper airplanes at her back. They put thumb tacks on her seat. The elder of the two Choquette brothers and Labonté were the best at sports: captains of the soccer and "ballon chasseur" teams. In the schoolyard they got their vengeance for what went on in class. They had so-called "accidents", a knee in the balls or a jab in the ribs, with the kids that they had sized up as timid or too brainy or, worst of all, teachers' stooges. They were everyone's heroes, except for those who got a knee in the balls. Choquette played a trick on me once. The day we were to hand in our essays on Pope John's death, he came up to my desk just before class (I was at the other end of the room, near the door); he stood there for a while, then picked up what I had written. He seemed very interested. It was my usual in memoriam essay, beginning "Pope John XXIII is dead, but the world shall not forget—" (A few years later I wrote a similar one on Churchill.) Choquette said he liked it, which seemed odd; then he added:

"You'll lose a lot of marks, because of that mistake."

"Mistake."

"Yeah, you got it wrong. He didn't die of cancer, it was syphilis." He had judged my innocence correctly: I didn't know what syphilis was, at the age of twelve. He was sixteen.

"What's syphilis?"

"Well it's . . . it's common among Popes."

I was suspicious. I had read 'cancer' in the newspapers and heard the word, distinctly, on the radio and television news reports. I knew that Choquette, apart from cheating and stealing from Hill's Candy Store and Delicatessen, and carving nude women on his desk with the point of his compass, was also a liar. He waited. "What are you waiting for? You going to change it, or aren't you?" I knew that I did not have the courage to call him a liar, not to his face. I watched his hands. They were much larger than mine, nearly all black with dirt. His fingernails were long. He could strangle me, I thought, if he wanted to.

"I don't know how to spell that word," I said. "I'll have to look it up in the dictionary first."

"It's spelled s-y-p-h-i-l-i-s."

I never thought he could spell so well. I made the necessary changes, erasing, and writing syphilis everywhere where cancer had been.

Missus Prudhomme then entered the room and demanded that our essays be handed in immediately, "On time, or else you get zero," which I got in any case. It was this essay that brought me out of my comfortable anonymity.

"Filth! Dirt! Blasphemy! Sacrilege! Your fingers should be cut off for this," she said, tearing my essay to shreds.

"You think you're funny, some joker, eh?"

"No," I said.

But she didn't believe me, and I received one of her karate slaps. All the while, in the rear corner, near the window, they were chuckling and throwing pieces of eraser at each other.

What bothered me, as I examined my sins, was that Choquette would not suffer for what he had done to me—and I envied him. This bothered me again, later, as I stood in the lineup to the confessional. Choquette did not believe in the things I believed in, and he would not suffer the consequences. I was sure of that much. He wouldn't go to a Catholic hell. A pagan one, perhaps; but that couldn't be as bad. We were standing in the same line and I could hear him chattering with his friends, just ahead of me, talking about sneaking off. Confession, communion, hell: it all meant nothing to him. "It's just a trick they use to get you to do things their way." "They" meant missus Prudhomme, the principal, his old man, too, maybe. It was his

truth.

When he went into the confessional he would probably tell the priest that he led a model life and everyone was taking advantage of him. And the priest would believe him. "It doesn't seem fair," I thought, looking across the church at the children and teachers, all waiting in line, and at those who had already gone and were at their benches kneeling in prayer, saying ten Hail Marys or three rosaries or whatever penance the priest had given them. "It doesn't seem fair," I almost said it aloud, but remembered missus Prudhomme standing behind me. I knew that questioning, doubting God's law, was also sinful—another sin.

"It doesn't seem fair," I thought it again.

from *The Spark Plug Thief*, by Marc Plourde

Beastliness!

Smoking and drinking are things that tempt some fellows and not others, but there is one temptation that is pretty sure to come to you at one time or another, and that you should be warned against. It is called in our schools "beastliness," and that is about the best name for it. Smoking and drinking and gambling are men's vices and therefore attract some boys, but this "beastliness" is not a man's vice; men have nothing but contempt for a fellow who gives way to it.

Some boys, like those who start smoking, think it a very fine and manly thing to tell or listen to dirty stories, but it only shows them to be little fools. Yet such talk and the reading of trashy books or looking at lewd pictures, are very apt to lead a thoughtless boy into the temptation of self-abuse. This is a most dangerous thing for him, for, should it become a habit, it quickly destroys both health and spirits; he becomes feeble in body and mind, and often ends in a lunatic asylum.

But, if you have any manliness in you, you will throw off such temptation at once; you will stop looking at the books and listening to the stories, and will give yourself something else to think about. Sometimes the desire is brought on by indigestion, or from eating too rich food, or from constipation. It can, therefore, be cured by correcting these, and by bathing at once in cold water, or by exercising the upper part of the body by arm exercises, boxing, etc. It may seem difficult to overcome the temptation the first time, but when you have done so once it will be easier afterwards. If you still have trouble about it, do not make a secret of it, but go to your Scoutmaster and talk it over with him, and all will come right. Bad dreams are another form of want of continence, which often come from sleeping in too warm a bed with too many blankets on, or from sleeping on your back; so try to avoid these causes.

from *The Canadian Boy Scout Handbook*, 1919

Said a youth from Saskatchewan
"You have something nobody can match you on.
   I'm referring my dear
   To a place at the rear
That it gives me such pleasure to pat you on."

   limerick quoted by John Robert Colombo

Dumb Indian Failure?

I came here a year ago and I am foreman for the hamlet and I really like the people and intend to stay a little longer. I was born in Fort Good Hope, three miles below, no doctors, birthday unrecorded, but sometime around 1940. According to the government I was supposed to be born July 11, and according to mom I was born August 11.

So I have two birthdays to celebrate. I like it that way.

When I was eight years old, the mission over at Aklavik opened up a school and some of us were told to go for a ride and you'll be back. Some of us were told you are going to the fish camp so, my brother and I, we jumped in and went to that Aklavik school.

Before I went to school the only English I knew was "hello" but when we got there we were told that if we spoke Indian they would whip us until our hands were blue on both sides. And we were also told that the Indian religion was superstitious and pagan. It made you feel inferior to the whites.

And the mail we used to get, it was read and what money was in it, which was not very much, was taken away from us, and then the mail was turned over to us if we knew how to read. It made me feel that all this time the native people had been wrong, but I was afraid to tell my parents. Now I realize that the native people were right all this time, passing their culture from generation to generation, to survive as Dene people.

The first day we got to school all our clothes were taken away and we didn't see them until we went home the following year, or until the school was over, and everybody was given a haircut which was a bald haircut.

We all felt lost and wanted to go home and some cried for weeks and weeks. I remember one Eskimo boy crying every night inside his blanket because he was afraid that the sister might come and spank him.

You were not allowed to talk to girls, not even your cousins. If you did, they would take your pants down and make you stand in front of the girls in your underwear until your face was red and you started crying. If you moved one step in any direction you would lose your only privilege, which was going to the movies. You went with the other students, but you faced the opposite direction. If you tried to turn around, well, upstairs to bed I guess.

You were not allowed to talk during meals or you were punished with a brush, again on the hands. And you had to wear different clothes during school hours and after school hours and right after you had to go outside and haul wood whether you were eight years old or not. And the wood was half green and you had to throw it down to the basement and pile it up.

Sometimes the weather was cold. Aklavik gets pretty cold, sixty below, but when you were told to play outside I remember that you were not to relieve yourself unless you went back into the room or back into the house and some were afraid to do that so they relieved themselves in their pants and took their parka and put their mitts inside; turned their head sideways to get out of the wind.

And if you lost your shoes you had to wear rags until you found your shoes.

Today, I think back on the hostel life and I feel ferocious. I feel a lot of anger inside of me. Between the ages of twelve and seventeen, I spent that in a hospital, TB, over in Aklavik. It wasn't fun either. Five years.

I decided to stay home and forget about education and try to see how I make out in the bush, living the way my mom and dad did. Having been away from home over in the hospital, I didn't know how to live in the bush. I felt lost. I didn't care about bush life too much because I was no longer able to live in the bush, so my uncle and my partner taught me to respect the land and tried to teach me about bush life. Well, anyway, uncle tried for something like six months and he gave up on me and told me to go back to my parents. I worked for D.O.T. digging out sewers and that was a pretty good job because that was my first job—$80 a month.

However, as springtime came, the sewers melted on their own and I got laid off. I remember that summer watching a white person driving a Cat in town, hauling logs and setting up a sawmill and I thought to myself, "Why can't I drive that Cat?" I am a failure as a dumb Indian anyway so I thought I'd change my culture and become white, and there was no way I could do that. But they taught me a little bit and that fall I decided to go back to school in Inuvik and they put me in an opportunity class where you are just taught to speak English and write. You are looked down on as just a dumb Indian who will not get anywhere.

After that school was over, my standing was grade six, but there is no paper. In 1960, I went

back to Good Hope along with other students. By that time most of my generation just spoke straight English because they had been forbidden to speak their own language in school. I felt confused, and I don't think I did anything that summer, so I decided to leave Good Hope again. This time, I felt, forever. I never wanted to go back there; I wanted to get out, and I had the opportunity to go to Yellowknife to go to school and study mechanics and there I found a very different system—government instead of missionary schools. I made up my mind that I didn't want to go back to Good Hope, so in the summer one of the teachers got me a job in Yellowknife with Wardair, $250 a month, and out of that I had to pay room and board, which was $90.

I used to stay just this side of the ball park, for those of you who know Yellowknife. From there I used to walk every morning to Old Town in order to save some cents for coffee. And I know for sure that there are 798 big square tiles, or sidewalks. I remember to this day. At this time they were pouring cement for the other side and just a couple of weeks ago I went back there and saw my initials.

Anyway, I spent about four and a half years in Yellowknife and I won the most outstanding award for mechanics, but there was no paper to prove it.

So I wasn't satisfied with going to school there. It was a good experience and when I graduated I thought, "Why not I go further, why not see the city?" So I had the opportunity to go down to Halifax, Nova Scotia. There there is another different system. You are more free, but they teach you geometry, physics, and all those Grade 12 subjects, and here I am just Grade 9.

At the same time I was getting letters from home, from mom and dad, and they told me my grandfather had died and I thought of that for a long time, what my older people were telling me, but I felt too far advanced, so I didn't bother. I kept on studying, and I didn't make out too good in the grades. So they put me in C.C.G.S. Labrador and I was the only Indian there and they nicknamed me "Mukluk".

I really felt—the parents writing to me, kept in the back of my mind—and I felt humiliated when they called me "Mukluk" so I turned to booze. My first drink was three bottles of beer and I got knocked out and I started picking up until I was

called "Mukluk" once more, from behind the back. I turned around and let the guy have it. I said, "That's it. I am returning back to Good Hope."

It was a long journey and it was good to see the sun setting. I knocked on mom and dad's door. I had a short haircut and tie and spit-polished shoes and dad looked at me and shook his head. I felt out of place there. I went up to the people I was working for and I slept there. I stayed there for a week and without seeing my parents I took off

back to Edmonton. In Edmonton I seen some of my old partners that I went to school with and they were down in the gutter where they hang out around 97th Street, Coffee Cup Inn and New Eddy and all of those places. All of these students, they had high hopes, but I think they lost their culture.

So I wandered around for a while and then I decided to return back to the north and this time really listen to my dad. Now the suit and tie has disappeared and I landed up a job with Rae Geophysical as a mechanic's helper.

I worked good for them so they sent me down to northern Alberta, High Level, June, 1967. The wages weren't that great. It was just sixteen dollars a day but at least I got a free trip out of it. Out there there was an oil rush at the time and in High Level the population was forty. Within a month it jumped to thirteen hundred. And we were doing field work for Shell Oil or some big company like that and sometimes I used to take the day off and drive out on the cut line and see how they operate. Sometimes they put canvass over the derricks, so the other companies won't spy on them. And they also had oil scouts going around with Land Rovers; some of them carried guns, I don't know what for. They tell me there are bears; in the fall the bears are hibernating anyway. I used to kid them by giving them a mud sample saturated with waste oil from my truck.

And then I went down to Rainbow Lake. By that time everything was completed, that was around the end of June or July, and they started building pipelines here and there. Some had signs saying gas, deadly gas, seeping out the side of the pipes.

At times I have seen some dead beavers around that area. I don't know, maybe they got killed by trucks or got poisoned by this gas; but of course I was the only Indian there and they asked me to skin it and I decided to return home and live the way my people had lived.

Dolphus Shae, from *The Past and Future Land*, by Martin O'Malley

About School

He always
He always wanted to explain things, but no one cared,
So he drew.

Sometimes he would just draw and it wasn't anything.
He wanted to carve it in stone or write it in the sky.
He would lie out on the grass and look up in the sky and it would
   be only the sky and things inside him that needed saying.

And it was after that that he drew the picture,
It was a beautiful picture. He kept it under his pillow and would
   let no one see it.
And he would look at it every night and think about it.
And when it was dark and his eyes were closed he could see it
   still.
And it was all of him and he loved it.

When he started school he brought it with him,
Not to show anyone, but just to have with him like a friend.

It was funny about school.
He sat in a square brown room, like all the other rooms,
And it was tight and close, and stiff.

He hated to hold the pencil and chalk, with his arm stiff and
   his feet flat on the floor, stiff, with the teacher watching
   and watching.

The teacher came and spoke to him.
She told him to wear a tie like all the other boys,
He said he didn't like them and she said it didn't matter.
After that he drew. And he drew all yellow and it was the way
   he felt about morning. And it was beautiful.

The teacher came and smiled at him. "What's this?" she said.
"Why don't you draw something like Ken's drawing?
   Isn't it beautiful?"

After that his mother bought him a tie and he always drew airplanes and rocket-ships like everyone else.
And he threw the old picture away.
And when he lay all alone looking at the sky, it was big and blue,
   and all of everything, but he wasn't anymore.

He was square and brown inside and his hands were stiff.
And he was like everyone else. All the things inside him that
   needed saying didn't need it anymore.

It had stopped pushing. It was crushed.
Stiff.
Like everything else.

Anonymous, from *I Am A Sensation*

Farewell to the Old School—Again

It has been sixteen years since I left the halls of Oakwood Collegiate for ever but, since the time I put in there was unquestionably the dreariest and most miserable period of my life, I still find it hard to ride a streetcar west, across the shabby wastelands of St. Clair Avenue, without feeling edgy. I want to get off the streetcar and go back east.

Five years I spent there, eternal seasons of penance for the sins of my boyhood. More than a thousand mornings, I entered the double doors at the north-east corner of this penitentiary that posed as a school and, as I remember things now, each day brought fresh exposés of my agonizing social incompetence, new cruelties from heartless girls, and more tortures at the hands of those grisly sadists who claimed to be teachers.

Now I know that Oakwood was as good a secondary school as most in Toronto and, indeed, better than many. Certainly, many of my classmates—specially the happy conformists who excelled at athletics and gloried year-round in their football reputations—loved old O.C.I. and wept when they had to leave. I freely concede that my hatred of Oakwood stemmed more from my own short-comings than from those of the school.

Still, I entered Oakwood Collegiate as a skinny, confused, ignorant twelve-year-old who was so shy he could neither sing nor talk out loud; and I left as a skinny, confused, ignorant seventeen-year-old who was so shy that he, too, could neither sing nor talk out loud.

I suppose the best thing the school did for me was to allow me to pass enough exams (though barely enough) to enter a small university in New Brunswick where, for the next three years, life was so bright I scarcely remembered the degradations at Oakwood.

Now, this morning, I happen to be at the corner of Oakwood and St. Clair and there, before me, is the terrible old hulk itself. Its bricks are brownish-yellow; they have the same complexion as the school disciplinarian had in my day. I feared him so much that for four years I could not bring myself to let my eyes meet his.

The trim on the windows is cream. Six signs tell me to keep off the grass. From the street, I can see clocks in three classrooms. They all say 9.07, and I know that in at least one of those classrooms, where the yellow overhead lights glow sickly above the blackboards, some skinny kid is already watching to see the longer hand click off one more minute in the path towards 3.30 in the afternoon.

He will stop clock-watching long enough to stare hotly and secretly at the girl whose skirt is shorter than anyone else's and, when he has worked himself into a fever of excitement, the teacher will ask him something he will never know how to answer. By then, it will be 9.12.

Standing out here on Oakwood Avenue, I can remember none of the good things about my high-school education, though I'm sure there must have been some. The bad things flood greedily back on their own: the compulsory swimming in a cold pool on the black afternoons of February, the compulsory military drill, with the big army rifle on your birdlike shoulder, the compulsory square dancing, the compulsory running around the gym in your underwear, the compulsory saying of "sir".

The compulsory sitting-down with thirty other baffled boys so that some chubby male teacher could wink slyly at us and, in the guise of a lecture on public health, give us the real low-down on girls and sex and all that stuff. There was one teacher who, when he was irritated by a few noisy pupils, would force the entire class to rise, sit down, rise, sit down—all in time to the raising and the lowering of his right index finger. There was a music teacher whose private tensions occasionally burst forth in awful fits of rage in which he'd smash records before the whole class.

There were teachers who seemed to have lost whatever inspiration they once thought their calling held, and were now maintaining some kind of self-respect by building a reputation among the students for ruthless sarcasm. There were, among teachers and students, occasional blatant examples of racial bigotry. There were the sneers, the insults, the loss of face, the fears, and, for some of us total high-school nonentities, there was the desperate, futile, and mute business of falling hopelessly in love roughly twenty times a year. These things, to me, were what old O.C.I. was all about.

But, of course, I must have been wrong. From some angles, the school looks almost pleasant this morning. There are more flowers blooming than there used to be. There's a big, clean, yellow-brick wing down on the south-western corner of the building, and it is new to me. There's a new football field with real sod and, already at 9.20, some goofy, rangy boys are out there in their gym shorts with a football. They seem to be having a pretty good time and, even if what I've said about Oakwood in the early fifties were the whole truth, the high schools of Toronto have surely changed for the better in the years since.

And besides, I'm thirty-three now, and no one, no vice-principal, no system, can make me go through those double doors to find out.

from *The Short Happy Walks of Max MacPherson*, by Harry Bruce

The Mountain

Philibert pressed the grease-smeared bell-button.

The door, as it opened, tore through the rancid shadow. He found himself facing a mountain. At the peak, in a cloud of black beard, was a face.

"I . . . I . . . I . . . read your ad in . . . *La Presse*."

"Knock me!" thundered the mountain.

Philibert thought he had misunderstood. The mountain repeated, in strangely-accented French this time, "Hit!"

The mountain got to its knees, the big head coming down to Philibert's level. The breath that came out of it stank like the exhaust fumes of a garbage truck.

"Hit me!"

The bristly hair and beard did not completely conceal the face, stained with blue scars.

"Are you afraid of to hit me?"

Philibert's fist struck at a rock of flesh. He ran to the staircase, afraid of being bashed into crumbs himself. The mountain rolled over behind him. He felt the vast breath in his back, its bitter warmth. Something seized him by the shoulder.

"You know to drive automobile?"

"Yes."

"You are brave. You are now private chauffeur of Boris Rataploffsky, the Ninth Vonder of Vorld."

* * *

Glowing with pride, the private chauffeur of the Ninth Wonder of the World sat behind the steering wheel of which he would henceforth be in charge. The cab of the truck would not contain his enormous boss; the giant travelled in the back, in a made-to-measure cabin. He had had a plywood box built on the chassis of the truck, the windows in the sides decorated with curtains made heavy by dirt. His throne was composed of two armchairs he had put together, nailed and sewed. The cabin was painted red with big white letters reading, "The Man with the Face of Steel"; smaller letters read, "Boris Rataploffsky"; and in bigger letters, "The Ninth Wonder of the World."

How could Philibert not be proud? The eyes of all Montreal were on his truck. People stopped and turned around to see it drive by. Cars slowed down, braked suddenly and risked collision to have a look at the truck carrying the Ninth Wonder of the World. It was the first time in his life that Philibert had felt proud.

A small bell rang behind his head. Boris Rataploffsky had given the signal. The truck stopped across from the Comme Chez Vous Tavern and Philibert ran to the back to open the doors. The Man with the Face of Steel got out with all the majesty of God the moment after Creation. When the huge foot touched the ground Montreal seemed to sink a little.

Boris Rataploffsky, preceded by Philibert, walked through the tavern. His big belly pitched and heaved above the tables and overturned chairs.

"Set us up!" Philibert ordered, surprised by his own authority.

The old waiter conscientiously brought several trays filled with glasses of beer and arranged them so that they covered the table. Around Philibert and the giant the most animated conversations fell silent.

Boris Rataploffsky, his little finger raised, drank glass after glass, row after row, very carefully, without spilling a drop of beer. He emptied them as though he were inhaling a whiff of air. No one else dared to drink. Life had come to a halt in the Comme Chez Vous Tavern. The giant's table was covered with empty glasses where the foam traced fine embroideries.

"Go on, my boy," said the giant.

Philibert adjusted his cap and stood up. "Ladies and gentlemen, mesdames et messieurs. You see before you the one, the only, the brilliant Boris Rataploffsky, the Man with the Face of Steel, the Ninth Wonder of the World, the Queen of England's favourite athlete. He gets a pension from the King of Brazil and the King of Hungary refused to pass over to the other side without seeing Boris Rataploffsky."

The giant coughed. When he was impatient, he coughed. Philibert hurried on.

"Your punches are like flea farts to this giant. Mesdames et messieurs, don't miss this chance to hit a giant. For one dollar you can hit him in the eye or on the mouth. Fifty cents and you can try for his nose and for a quarter you get to hit him anywhere else on the face. Careful! Don't get hurt! Step right up! Pay here. We won't be back. Hit the giant! Pansies, call for your mummies!"

In the cushions of his flesh, Boris Rataploffsky was dreaming.

"Come on, come on! Ladies and gentlemen! The giant won't hurt you. His steel face feels no pain."

"I'm going to wake up that big ciboire of a pile of dead meat."

The brave man paid his dollar and proudly

rolling up his sleeves, he walked up to face the Man with the Face of Steel. He caressed his fist with his other hand, stamping like a horse about to kick. He straightened out his fist, clenched it again, tightened it, made it hard and sharp with all his might. All at once he hit the giant. The frightened customer was already far away. The giant slept on.

Philibert's hand was filled with bills and fists fell in an avalanche on the unfeeling mountain. Nothing disturbed the shadows of the face.

The customers hit until they had exhausted themselves. They had less and less strength. They laughed. The giant's thoughts were elsewhere.

Suddenly a little drop of blood was visible in his eyebrow.

"Baptême!" Philibert panicked. "It isn't true he's got a face of steel."

He yelled, gesturing broadly, "OK, that's it. All over now."

The Ninth Wonder of the World left the tavern behind Philibert, whose pockets were heavy with the money they had accumulated. Without a word he got into his cabin in the red truck with the flat springs.

Philibert put the take into his outstretched hands. A smile flickered in the beard. Philibert closed the door of the cabin.

* * *

Philibert broke a dozen eggs, sliced a salami, added onions, red and green peppers and cream, mixed it all up in a saucepan with his hands and then cooked it on the gas-stove, which was no longer sticky since he had cleaned it.

The Ninth Wonder of the World ate the omelette with the enthusiasm of a child. Philibert would never get used to his strength. When the Man with the Face of Steel spoke, Philibert shuddered as the house of his childhood had shuddered in the wind.

"Monsieur Rataploffsky, I've got an idea."

"An idea? Show me it."

The photograph on the opposite page is of Louis Cyr, legendary Canadian strongman who lived from 1863 to 1912. At the peak of his strength he stood five feet, ten and a half inches tall and weighed 315 pounds. To many knowledgeable Canadians, Louis Cyr remains the strongest man in history.

Philibert explained: it was a mistake for the Ninth Wonder of the World to display himself in half-empty taverns and miserable restaurants where the neighbours got together for a smoke. Only the great arenas were worthy of an attraction as spectacular as the Man with the Face of Steel. Instead of putting on his show several times a day, Boris Ratapoffsky could make more money by exhibiting himself in the big arenas, before delirious crowds.

The giant applauded.

"You're my man. You'll be my manacher."

"O.K. And from now on my name is Phil. Monsieur Phil. Mister Phil. Manager! Baptême! I can't believe myself."

* * *

From spring until fall the red truck took the Ninth Wonder of the World from Montreal to Gaspé, from Rouyn to Sherbrooke. Everywhere he was given a royal welcome. On his manager's advice, he wore a gold cape with "The Man with the Face of Steel" embroidered on it. In the cities he was surrounded by children and pimply-faced adolescents and old men. They were all the same age before Boris Ratapoffsky, as they pushed and jostled, marvelled and bickered, trying to get a chance to touch the Ninth Wonder of the World. They were ecstatic, doubtful; they argued. If the giant raised his hand they stepped back.

Phil always walked ahead of his boss. He busied himself pretending to chase away the importunate. He told them on every possible occasion that just the night before he had refused to sell the giant for the sum of three thousand dollars to American interests. "We already sold too many of our natural resources to foreigners," he would conclude.

All along the highways linking the arenas, through the poor, interminable forests or the flat infinite plains, the giant sang. Phil didn't understand the words of his strange songs that made the roof of his cabin quiver, but he sensed that they were words of joy.

* * *

In the middle of the ring, whose ropes had been painted white for the occasion, the Man with the Face of Steel stood motionless under the bombardment of fists. The volcano was sleeping.

"Step right up!" shouted Phil over the loudspeakers. "Here's your chance to hit a bigger man than you are. Right this way!"

All around the ring there were children, pallid labourers, muscular lumberjacks, coughing schoolboys, salesmen with slicked-down hair and distinguished ladies; they grew impatient or startled or placed bets. They climbed into the ring, saluted the crowd, and hit. Joyous applause. Each blow was greeted by a delighted outburst from the crowd. They paid and began all over again, twice, three times. Their pleasure grew. The distinguished ladies kept their rings on their fierce little hands.

At times a stain would appear on the eyelid of the Face of Steel. An old wound reopening or a badly-healed scab. A little blood would flow. Then the fists would let loose, attacking the Face of Steel on all sides. hitting as though you had to destroy to live, as if the giant's face were a prison wall. Their strength increased with each blow. The giant coughed slightly and the fists persisted as though they were attacking a vanquished fawn.

There were shouts of joy and dancing in the shaking stands. Phil could not pick up all the bills that flew around his head like crazy birds. He was powerless to control the crowd. Like a nation of ants they swarmed into the ring, ready to assault the too kindly giant. There were ten of them hitting without let-up, and without paying.

Phil shouted, "Pay right here! Pay here! It's cheap!"

Suddenly the Ninth Wonder of the World stood up, yelling as though he were spitting fire. Before the shock-waves struck the walls he picked up a big man and threw him among the spectators, where he was crushed like an egg. The giant had already grabbed three other men; these he threw at the ceiling. When the three unfortunates had dropped to the floor the angry mountain fell on them with the force of a landslide.

The crowd was silent.

Women wept.

Lovers let their arms fall from their girlfriends' waists.

The giant came up to Phil, putting a hand as heavy as an ox on the boy's shoulder. Blood was streaming from his mouth.

"You are good boy," he grunted. "Don't forget."

Big tears mingled with his blood.

The Man with the Face of Steel climbed out of the ring and went towards one of the exits. He knocked over everything in his path, crushing it like grass.

The bleachers were on the edge of a gentle lake. The giant walked along the shore and got into a rowboat that sank almost out of sight under the burden of his enormous weight.

Phil called, "Wait for me!"

The giant didn't listen. He rowed, but the submerged boat moved along painfully, an island adrift. The giant put the oars inside the boat. Gently, it came to a stop.

Then very slowly the Ninth Wonder of the World got up and let himself fall into the water. He didn't try to swim. He was no longer a giant but a man.

His body was found by a child swimming in the last rays of the sun.

"Who was Boris Rataploffsky?"

"What country did he come from?"

Phil didn't know. He was too drunk, they said. Phil assured them that he knew nothing of the giant's life.

He replied, "What's the use of being a giant on the earth? What's the use of being an ordinary man?"

They laughed.

Sitting in the water that lapped at the sand, Philibert wept.

from the novel, *Philibert Is It the Sun*, by Roch Carrier

Youngsters

One thing that puzzles me is all this stuff we read in the papers and hear about over the radio about the youngsters nowadays. You'd think when you're listening to it or reading about it that the youngsters growin' up today are an awful crowd and they're a lot worse than we older fellows were when we were their age.

Like I said, it puzzles me. I've got to believe it, or I *suppose* I have. After all, I don't suppose they'd print it in papers or talk it over radios if it wasn't true. But when I look at the young boys and maidens growin' up today in Pigeon Inlet and compare 'em with what we were like when we were their age, I'm inclined to think that they're not half as bad as we were. Of course, I'm only talkin' about places like Pigeon Inlet—perhaps in big places like St. John's it's different. Still—it puzzles me.

For one thing, the youngsters here nowadays are dressed up better—and that makes a difference—especially to the little girls. All you got to do with one of them is tell her what a pretty dress she's got on and she'll try to keep out of mischief so as to keep it lookin' pretty. But it makes a difference to the boys, too. They dress better when they go to school, and I believe it helps to keep them cleaner and tidier. What a difference from when me and my brother Ki used to go to school 40-odd years ago. I remember one day my hands were so dirty that, when the teacher went to cane me, like she did most days, I was almost ashamed to hold my hand out. So I picked out the hand that I figured wasn't quite as dirty as the other and stuck it out for the teacher to take a whack at. You should have seen the look that came over her face, "Mose Mitchell," she said, "aren't you ashamed to have a hand so dirty as that?" Of course I hung my head and tried to look ashamed as best I could, and said "Yes, Miss." Then she said, "Mose, that's the dirtiest hand I''ve ever seen on a boy. In fact," she said, "if you can find me a dirtier hand than that in the school, I won't cane you."

Well, there was only one thing for me to do, and I did it. "Yes, Miss," I said, "I know where there's a dirtier hand than that in the school." "I can't believe it, Mose," said she. "Where is it?" "Here it is, Miss," said I, and I stuck out the other one. She took one look at it and let me off.

Another thing about the boys nowadays. Not only are they a bit tidier and go to school oftener—on account of the family allowance, of course—but, when they're in school, they're a lot better behaved than they used to be. Why, a few years ago, whenever you passed by a school you'd swear the sides were goin' to burst out. But now it's different. You pass along by a school now and only for the bicycles out by the door, you'd hardly know there was anybody inside. The head teacher here is only a little, quiet fellow, not much bigger than some of the schoolboys, but he says he never has any trouble. He says the boys seem to like being in school and learn their lessons without too much trouble.

Oh, my! What a difference! When I think of the devilment that used to go on in school forty years ago, when me and my brother Ki were boys. Bad as I was, I think Ki was even worse, and I believe I've just got time to tell you a story about him. Like I told you before, Ki was two years older than I was, and he used to get a lickin' in school almost every day. Then he'd manage to arrange it so I got a lickin' too and so I wouldn't be able to go home and tell tales about him. The teacher used to blame Ki for just about everything bad that was done in school and generally the teacher was right.

Well, one day, something really bad happened. Somebody stole fifty cents off the teacher's desk during recess time. The teacher was a big husky man—and he looked hard at Ki out of the corner of his eye. Then he said, "Now, this is serious. This is the worst thing ever happened in all my long years of school-teachin'. It's so bad that I don't want to know who did it. But whoever did it has got to give back the fifty cents. Now," said the teacher, "here's what we're going to do. I'm going to take all the sawdust out of these old chalk boxes and put it into the coal bucket. Then I'm going to hold up the coal bucket and each one of you must take your turn and put your fist down among the sawdust and bring it up again. So whoever took the fifty-cent piece will leave it among the sawdust and we'll never know who took it."

So we all lined up and walked past the teacher, put our hands in among the sawdust and took 'em out again. Then the teacher emptied the sawdust out on the floor and searched among it. There was no sign of the fifty-cent piece.

"Now children," he said, "this is more serious. You had your chance to put it back without anyone being the wiser. Now I've got to know who took it."

At that, a little girl burst out crying. "Please, sir," she said, "I took it."

"You took it," said the teacher. "Yes, sir," said she. "Well then," said he, "Why didn't you put it back among the sawdust?

"Please, sir," said she, "I put it back among the sawdust." The teacher looked puzzled for a minute until he took a glance at the grin on Ki's face. Yes, you've guessed it. Ki had it. He handed it out to the teacher with a few grains of sawdust stickin' to it.

Of course, the teacher give Ki a lickin' for takin' the fifty-cent piece out of the sawdust after the little girl had put it in, but he didn't lick Ki very hard. I think he knew Ki only did it for devilment and that actually Ki wouldn't steal anything to save his life. 'Cause if Ki had been that kind of fellow, he wouldn't be where he is today in New Brunswick.

from *The Chronicles of Uncle Mose*, by Ted Russell

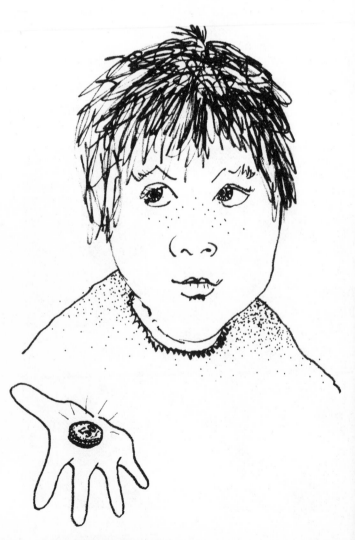

The west that was . . .

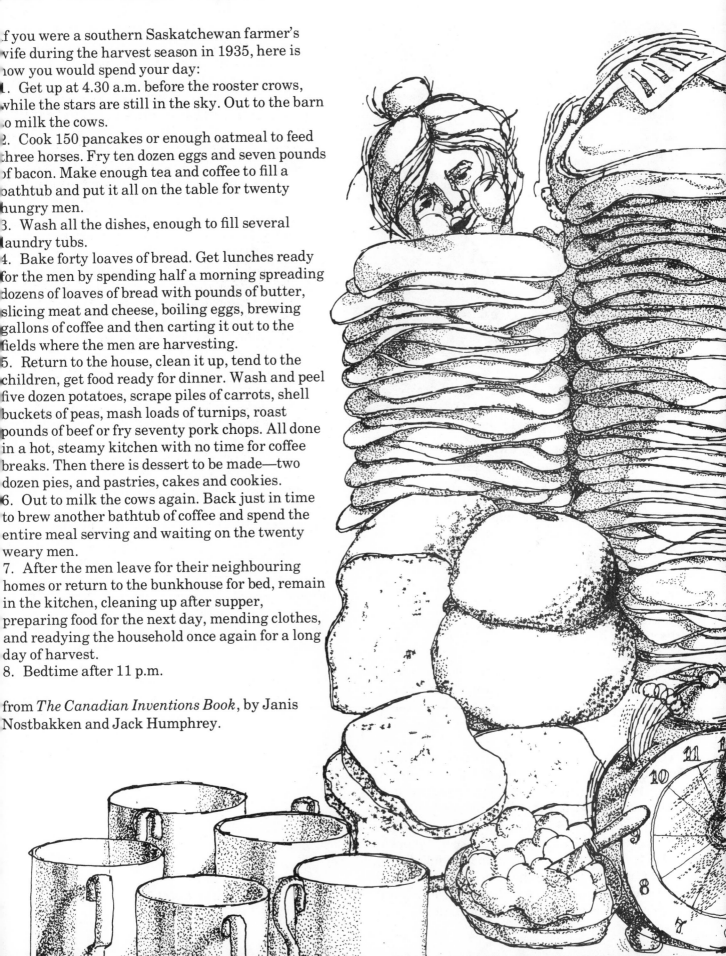

If you were a southern Saskatchewan farmer's wife during the harvest season in 1935, here is how you would spend your day:

1. Get up at 4.30 a.m. before the rooster crows, while the stars are still in the sky. Out to the barn to milk the cows.

2. Cook 150 pancakes or enough oatmeal to feed three horses. Fry ten dozen eggs and seven pounds of bacon. Make enough tea and coffee to fill a bathtub and put it all on the table for twenty hungry men.

3. Wash all the dishes, enough to fill several laundry tubs.

4. Bake forty loaves of bread. Get lunches ready for the men by spending half a morning spreading dozens of loaves of bread with pounds of butter, slicing meat and cheese, boiling eggs, brewing gallons of coffee and then carting it out to the fields where the men are harvesting.

5. Return to the house, clean it up, tend to the children, get food ready for dinner. Wash and peel five dozen potatoes, scrape piles of carrots, shell buckets of peas, mash loads of turnips, roast pounds of beef or fry seventy pork chops. All done in a hot, steamy kitchen with no time for coffee breaks. Then there is dessert to be made—two dozen pies, and pastries, cakes and cookies.

6. Out to milk the cows again. Back just in time to brew another bathtub of coffee and spend the entire meal serving and waiting on the twenty weary men.

7. After the men leave for their neighbouring homes or return to the bunkhouse for bed, remain in the kitchen, cleaning up after supper, preparing food for the next day, mending clothes, and readying the household once again for a long day of harvest.

8. Bedtime after 11 p.m.

from *The Canadian Inventions Book*, by Janis Nostbakken and Jack Humphrey.

Childbirth

Early in the next spring, I was expecting a child. Often I would run and bury myself in the deep prairie grass and weep for my mother. How were babies born, anyway? The present-day girl with her comprehensive knowledge of life was a far cry from my girlhood, where we were literally sheltered from that type of knowledge. Mother sent me two volumes from England, *Advice to a Wife* and *Advice to a Mother* and studying the illustrations I became more terror-stricken but I wouldn't have thought of showing that fact or of discussing it.

The nearest doctor lived at Humboldt, fifty miles away. My husband had notified him that we would need him around a certain date and one of the McCabe boys had promised to take a fast team and sleigh when we would put up a flag as a signal or a lantern at night, and go and get him. But we reckoned without the weather. For three days a wild blizzard raged and we seemed to be cut off in a white world of quietness. It was hardly safe for Duke to find his way the short distance to the stable. The path was entirely obliterated. When the storm first started, he piled hay and blocks of snow for the cattle, to last them for a few days. On the fourth day the sun shone bright and clear. The cattle were let out of the stables and floundered around in the deep snow, their nostrils emitting

steam-like breath on the frosty air. I muffled up in a fur coat and was glad to be outside too, and for fun helped Duke pitch hay into the stalls. I felt lighter, happier, as though some awful load were lifted and we were very gay at my laborious efforts. That night I awoke in an agony of pain. Arousing Duke, he lit the lamps and put on a huge tub of water to heat. It was snowing and so no use to put up the lantern. As I was wracked with agony, Duke held my hands and in between the knife-like pains, I would let out peals of laughter in a wild, excited way. Later, I remember Duke, seen through the haze of the lamp light with sleeves rolled up and perspiration rolling down his face, walking between the book *Advice to a Wife* which was propped up on the table as he followed the processes of birth in the book, and actually delivered the child, a perfect boy, who protested lustily at his entrance into the world.

Duke wrapped up the child and laid it beside me. He knelt down beside the bed and put both hands around my face as gently as a woman, saying, "Christy, I don't have to tell you to be brave, for there is no one like you in the world, but I'll have to leave you to get someone to go for the doctor, for the rest is a doctor's work, though I'll have to take the risk if I can't get him." He left me, going out into the early dawn on skis. I heard later that when he reached our neighbour's threshhold, he fell across in a dead faint. He came back to me and we waited patiently for the doctor, who was also to bring a nurse. As the hours passed Duke came to me and said "Christy, I'm afraid I'll have to take a chance and remove. . . ." Before he finished speaking we heard the faint tinkle of sleighbells and soon the doctor, nurse and the driver entered. The doctor had to thaw out before he could touch me and when he did it was far worse than the actual birth. Duke showed the strain as he almost sobbed, "Thank God, Doctor, you arrived in time." The doctor congratulated Duke on his skill. The memory of that night has never been erased from my mind. I know the meaning of the word "man".

Edith Lazonby, from *Salt of the Earth*, by Heather Robertson

Like An Eskimo

It was about 1936 when the igloo part came in. Oh God, it was cold, day after day, and down around 45 degrees (*below zero*) but we couldn't know because a radio was an expensive thing in them days and getting into town took enough out of a man without going around and asking about temperature. The house never was that much. Wood, no insulation then, fire burner in the kitchen and wood hard to get, and my wife said she was just waiting for the next big wind to blow us into the gully. The frost was an inch thick on the windows everywhere and the boys and me only left the house to get wood and feed the stock because we'd laid in a lot of Russian thistle and stinkweed and barley and wheat which never came to a head that summer before at all but was kind of a feed for the six cows I kept. People around said six cows was too many but I've always felt cows was something to fall back on. It's the countryman in me.

About the igloo. We'd got to know this lad in Regina who worked on the railroad and he drove down some time in January bringing some National Geographics for the children and a can of pipe tobacco for me and a bottle. Gavin had been in the Arctic for years and he kept looking around the house not saying anything and then my wife said, "I know, Gavin, God didn't, God never meant people to live like this in this cold," and she started to cry. First time she'd ever cried front of the children.

Gavin started telling us that an Eskimo lived better in an igloo than we did, warmer, cozier, and then he turned to little Mary, she was just ten, and he asked if she would like to live in an igloo. She nodded yes and Gavin got up and told me to come out and me and the boys went with him and he walked over the gully behind the house and he asked how deep the snow was and I cast an eye on it and I said it was at least nine feet deep. I remember him saying, "Deep enough," and then he said, "Wind has packed her down like granite. She'll do."

Well, my friend, we got shovels and we started to dig a tunnel, about yea high, I could just bend over in it, about five feet, and he went on to explain that the mouth faced away from the wind. You know about snow, I guess. She's a fine insulation. We took turns digging into the big drift and about ten feet in, Gavin said he'd take over and he turned a corner and the snow, in chunks like concrete, came flying out and he said

he'd now build the house. Mary came out with coffee and we knelt around in the tunnel and it was quite warm.

To make a long story short, we built, or we dug, a big room about ten by twelve feet and five or so feet high. The boys went out to the barn and brought back horse blankets and grain sacks and straw and we laid them on the snow floor. Gavin got a broom and went up on top and said, "If I break through, she's no good anyway," but it held and he poked about six holes through with the broom and got empty tin cans and punched jagged big holes in them and set them over the holes and got them turned so the wind wouldn't blow down them.

By this time Jack and Harry were real excited and they went out to the barn and lugged in boards and we made some beds and they brought blankets from the house and so we had beds. Does all this sound loonie? Well, it all happened. Of course we brought out several lanterns and that made the place light and we had a little oil stove we set up on a board platform and they all provided plenty of heat and the stove was for cooking. We brought out all our food and magazines and everything we needed and we just walked away from that house.

Food? No, we never wanted for it. I had six dollars coming in every month, the relief, and Mary's aunt was sending her ten every month by money order and two of our cows were still milking and there were a few hens. We did fine. Mind you, nothing fancy, but better than an awful lot of people who wasn't living in an igloo. I'd buy dried beans and dried apples and salt pork, sugar and coffee, corn meal, lard, flour, bread of course, and strawberry jam and we had our bacon. We killed quite a few chickens so we had chicken soup and stew and we were fine. We were warm, our igloo was the easiest thing to keep clean, and I guess it was between 35 and 45 below for a long time that winter and we never felt it at all. Cozy as cooties.

Going to the bathroom was a problem until I carved out a small biffy in the snow and we'd just cover it up. The thing I liked about an igloo was the maintenance, it was so simple. The boys just had to make sure that if there was new snow then that the tin cans over the air and smoke holes had to be cleaned and fixed again. A buffalo rug over the entrance and a horse blanket over the second entrance, into the big room, was all we needed. We were doing fine.

In about three weeks the kids decided to go back to school and pretty soon we were having visitors. They were bringing their chums home, and by golly, soon the old folks would be coming. Kept us going just making coffee for them. Sometimes one of them would come up with a bottle of his own homebrew and we'd sing and life wasn't too bad, except that we all was stony broke. I guess you could say we were celebrities. The police even came by one afternoon. They weren't looking for trouble, but they sure were curious. They wrote a report but nothing came of it. Oh yes, something did. The Regina newspaper heard of it and they sent a man down, quite a way you understand, but by that time it was getting into spring, sometime in March, and the snow house was drippy and we had moved back into the house. One thing about igloos, once they start to drip they're just no damn good. But we lived in her for about six or seven weeks and they were good times. Kids didn't have colds and they did their lessons at night without being asked and the wife and I got along better and we ate well and Gavin came down to see us

once a few weeks after we'd moved in and he looked around and stayed the night and next morning he said we could show an Eskimo a thing or two.

That year our little farm got some rain at the right time and the wind stopped blowing so, and there was a bit of a crop. But we decided this was no life anyway and we went into Regina. But the kids, Harry was killed with the war, but Mary and Jackie, when they write, which is seldom, they always say did I remember what it was like, Dad, living in an igloo. I sure do, and they've never forgot it either.

as told to Barry Broadfoot in *Ten Lost Years*

The farmer is king, oh, the farmer is king,
And except for his wife and daughter,
Who boss him around, he runs the thing,
Come drought, come hell or high water

Paul Hiebert

.... and The West That Is

The knife makes a small cracking sound as it cuts through the vein and breaks the neck. The lamb grunts and makes frantic running motions with its trussed legs as the blood spurts out and runs down its side. Small, mangy black cats scuffle in from the dark corners of the barn and crouch in the straw in an expectant circle. Rolling its eye balefully upwards, breathing hard, the lamb raises and lowers its head. Close beside the lamb, the dog Ringo leans forward occasionally and tenderly licks the blood from the wound. "Sheep," says Gordon Taylor, "take forever to die."

We wait in silence. The barn is warm and cozy, the air heavy with manure. Old pieces of leather harness and rope and baler twine hang from the low beams; sweet straw piled high in the stalls is bright yellow where sunlight streaming in the door and through cracks in the weathered boards falls on it. The dozen sheep penned up outside bleat loudly.

The lamb begins to thrash convulsively. "Come

on, boy," says Gordon anxiously, leaning over it in his big white paper apron, "come on." The lamb's eye is big with fear.

"You can't shoot a sheep. The brain is so far back it's hard to find. It's not very humane to do it this way, I suppose, but it's the only way. I can do a lamb in twenty minutes; this one will take longer because he's bigger."

When the lamb is dead, he hooks it to a block and tackle and strings it upside down to a rafter. With a quick stroke, he slits it down the belly and expertly skins it. He tosses the hide aside into the straw and dung.

"You know how much a sheepskin is worth? Ten cents. They sell for thirty dollars in The Bay in Saskatoon. I've got a pile of fifty of them going mouldy out in the yard; it doesn't pay us to skin them."

He ties up the esophagus and cuts off the penis. "A sheep is the only animal you can do this with," he says; "usually the urine comes pouring out." Another stroke and the guts come spilling onto the ground; the cats fight over the liver and the dog sniffs experimentally around the stomach.

"You get sort of hardened to it after a while," says Gordon, hacking off the head. "Cold blooded.

It's my livelihood. A lot of farmers won't do this, get their hands dirty butchering."

He takes a rag from a little plastic pail of water and wipes the carcass lightly with it. After the lamb has hung for an hour, Gordon lugs it to the station wagon. Later he will drive it to the butcher in town, who will cut it into chops.

"I killed the ram, the ugly one," he announces in the kitchen with a big smile.

A few hours later, he goes back to the barn, shovels the guts into a wheelbarrow, and dumps them out in the pasture. "The dogs and cats thrive on them," he says. "We even get coyotes coming in for them, magpies too. If there's anything left in the spring, I bring it back and bury it in the manure pile."

The ram will feed the Taylors for 25 meals.

Gordon and Norma Taylor farm 1,200 acres near Landis, Saskatchewan, about seventy-five miles west of Saskatoon, an average-sized farm for Saskatchewan. They own 800 acres and rent the rest from a neighbour who's moved to the city. They grow wheat, oats, and barley—the same as everybody else in the area—and Gordon keeps a breeding herd of 150 ewes. Their farm is worth $100,000, but the Taylors are poor. In 1971 net income from the farm was $2,900 and Gordon earned another $500 working part-time in a grain elevator. But after they paid $1,200 in taxes on their land, they were left with $2,200 to support themselves and their five children.

"As far as money is concerned," says Gordon, "it's non-existent."

Like all family farms on the prairies, the Taylors are slowly being squeezed into bankruptcy. They have dug their fingernails into the soil and hang on with fierce determination. The Taylors are fighting for their lives, and the struggle absorbs every ounce of their energy and intelligence. Behind their natural cheerfulness lies a strain of desperation which often brings them close to tears.

Thirty Canadian farmers leave the land every day. They have cut each other's throats. For twenty-five years prairie farmers have fought each other tooth and claw, have scrapped over more land, bigger machinery, and more bushels of wheat, with each man determined to be richer than his neighbour down the road, until the survivors find themselves impoverished. Over 150,000 farmers have been pushed off the land in western Canada in the interests of efficiency; the result is, in Manitoba Premier Ed Schreyer's words, "a rural slum."

The majority of prairie farmers are poor; even rich farmers are poor by urban standards. In 1971, which was considered a good year, the average Saskatchewan farmer made $4,616—half what an urban construction worker makes every year. In 1970, the year of the most recent agricultural depression, the average farm income 'across the prairies was $2,500—less than a farm family would make on welfare.

Saskatchewan farmers are relatively worse off than they were in the Thirties; for now, everyone is rich except them. Inflation is forcing them out. Gordon Taylor sells $9,000 worth of produce every year, but expenses eat up $6,000. Every year his margin of profit gets a little smaller. "You have one good year and two bad ones," he says. "You come up again, but you never come up quite so high." The squeeze is a deliberate policy of the Trudeau government, which hopes that within another generation only a quarter of Canada's 400,000 farmers will still be on the land. Farmers like the Taylors, who hang on, have been pushed back to a subsistence living close to that their grandfathers scratched off a homestead.

The Taylors live in the old stucco house where Gordon was born. The house has grown wrinkled and middle-aged along with him. The stucco is brown and stained, and there are patches of tarpaper where Gordon has replaced the windows. The house is on a little knoll; the land at the back slopes abruptly to a slough, where the sheep pasture in the summer. The unpainted farm buildings are grey with age.

There are big holes in the Taylors' living room walls where the plaster has fallen away. The old-fashioned wallpaper is mottled brown and streaked with water stains. Sunlight filters in through white plastic curtains with blue flowers. On a black-and-white television in the corner stand colour photographs of all the children. Out in the porch, next to two freezers, are cardboard boxes full of new wallboard and ceiling tile for the living room. "The wallboard isn't what I wanted," says Norma, "but we got it for half price."

A sign in Norma's kitchen says: "My kitchen is clean enough to be healthy and dirty enough to be happy." The floor heaves and sags, the pattern is worn off the linoleum, and the walls have fingerprints on them. A big sign on the freezing compartment of the ancient refrigerator says: "Do Not Open!" It's a homemade, helter-skelter house with rooms in unexpected places; walls have been put up and knocked down to fit the needs of the people living in it. Everybody uses the back door.

A little path leads from the back door of the house to the biffy. It's a two-holer, with one hole directly facing the door if you want to look out into the yard, and the other in the corner for privacy. The wooden covers for the holes fit loosely, because the boards of the seat have been worn round and smooth. On hot days the biffy hums with flies, and the stench is heavy.

The Taylors installed their first flush toilet in the spring of 1972. They still use the outhouse after a heavy rain, when mud seeps into the well and the indoor toilet fills up with black water. Next winter, Gordon plans to put in the new lavender bathtub and sink that are still crated up out in the porch. Gordon does all the work himself, because he can't afford to hire a carpenter. He borrowed the money to buy the fixtures from the credit union in Landis.

"It's ridiculous," says Norma. "After twenty years, we're still putting the *plumbing* in. You get a house in town that doesn't have water and sewer and it's condemned."

Farmer Needs the Rain

The Taylors have been farming for twenty-one years, ever since they were married. In only five of those years have they earned enough to pay income tax. For seven years, Gordon drove a school bus to earn enough money to buy groceries.

His bind is simple and universal. It costs him $17 to grow an acre of wheat that he then sells for $11. The price of wheat in the summer of 1972 is less than it was in 1951, the year he started farming.

The Taylors live off the land. Their farm is a family commune; there is no distinction on it between life and work. Their relationship with the land is profound, primordial; the farm is a reflection of them, the fruit of their labour. Gordon goes about his primitive, menial tasks with joy, a sense of tenderness and responsibility. He would have been at home with Abraham and Isaac: he is a husbandman.

from *Grass Roots*, by Heather Robertson

The day of my birth I was helpless and my mother took care of me although she was not able to do it alone, there was some one to help her take care of me and I lived. Today, although a man, I am as helpless before this Court, in the Dominion of Canada and in this world as I was helpless on the knees of my mother the day of my birth. The North West is also my mother, it is my mother country, and although my mother country is sick and confined in a certain way, there are some from Lower Canada who came to help her to take care of me during her sickness, and I am sure that my mother country will not kill me more than my mother did. . . .

> Louis Riel, in a speech
> defending himself in Regina
> July 31, 1885

"A man without land is nobody. Remember that, Duddel."

> *The Apprenticeship of Duddy
> Kravitz* by Mordecai Richler

Ooh the farmer needs the rain
And the farmer needs the heat
Need it in the proper order
To grow a field of wheat
But when the wind keeps a blowin'
Blowin' everything away
You can bet your boots
The farmer's gonna pay

The government is helpful
They tell you what to plant
You take it into town
They turn around and say no thanks
And then the cops pull you over
Right in front of the bank
Just wanna see if you got
Purple gas in your tank

    An' then the credit man comes to see you
    At the break of day
    He might have to take the truck
    'Cause you can't pay right away
    And you look towards the sky
    All your praying in vain

    We got a lotta bills to pay
    When do we get a break
    The farmer needs
    The farmer needs the rain

Well it's another dry sundown
Navy blue and red
Linda's out sellin' Avon
And the kids are tucked in bed
The radio is cracklin'
An' the tractor's in the shed
And I'm thinkin' 'bout some things
my father said

He said
The farmer needs the rain
And the farmer needs the heat
Need it in the proper order
To grow a field of wheat
But when the wind keeps a blowin'
Blowin' everything away
You can bet your boots
The farmer's gonna pay.

Bim, from his record *Raincheck On Misery*

Some Place to Live, My Sons

A CBC Radio Script

It is less than a week now since the four of us from this program who went to Newfoundland returned to our home base, and though I cannot speak for them, I suspect that they all have some of the same feeling I have this morning, which I can only describe as a sort of homesickness. For me, this is a rare phenomenon. As I'm sure I've said before on this program, I've spent a lot of my life, both before I became a journalist and, partly because of that, after I went into writing and broadcasting for a living, travelling around Canada. A list of the places I've lived or worked over the years, including the thirteen months or so since this program began, sounds remarkably like the lyrics to a song by the Travellers. Toronto, or at least southern Ontario, is my home, of course, and while that doesn't necessarily mean I think it's the best part of the country — as a matter of fact, I don't — it does mean it's where I live. Yet I still have felt, everywhere I've gone, *at home* — in a way I could not, for instance, in Cleveland, Ohio, or Bayswater, Georgia, or Kingston, Surrey, England.

I once wrote a long essay in *Maclean's* magazine about how Saskatchewan was the most Canadian part of Canada — yet even that doesn't mean I think it's the best. What is the best part? Or, for that matter, what is the most Canadian part of Canada? I'm sure I don't know, but I do know that I have never enjoyed a week of travelling quite so much, or, for that matter, felt so instantly at home, as I did in Newfoundland last week. I haven't said anything about this until now because I wanted to make sure that when I talked about Newfoundland I was not still high on the hospitality of the people we met there or the sheer and — for me, at least — surprising physical beauty of the place. But since we left I've been kind of turning over in my mind what happened to us there and what seemed to us at least to make Newfoundland a province not like the others.

As I turn that thought over, the picture that keeps coming to my mind is a group of people, ourselves from Upper Canada, but mostly Newfoundlanders, sitting around over a glass of rum one afternoon — not screech, either, *rum* — and just gabbing. The gist of this conversation was about the difference between pre-Confederation and post-Confederation Newfoundland. Confederation, for God's sake. To those of us who grew up in other parts of the country, or indeed in other countries, Confederation is a dull, dry, abstract word that conjures up, if it conjures up anything, tricky and uninteresting questions on history examinations, or the formal picture of a group of men, all

obviously holding too still too long for an artist. But to Newfoundlanders who are no older than I am, it is living politics, or at the very least living and very recent history. They *experienced* it, during the long, bitterly fought debates of the 1940s, and on all of their lives — from a lawyer I talked to in Cornerbrook, who many people think will one day be premier of Newfoundland, to a tough and gentle old lady who lives by social assistance in the outport of Ferryland, and who entertained us for an afternoon — on all of their lives it had a direct and specific effect. For us, history; for Newfoundland, reality. And because of that, I think that Newfoundland, which is at once our youngest and our oldest province, has a sense of its own past and traditions that the rest of us lack. I guess in a way I envy Newfoundlanders that sense, but even in a week it is possible to share enough of it with them to carry it around for quite a while. Newfoundland may have got the baby bonus by joining Confederation in 1949; but the rest of us, I'd suggest, got something quite a lot more important from them.

Someone asked me yesterday if, because of the way the program has been moving around — and will continue to move, incidentally, beginning in Alberta early next month — if because of that I had a particular vision of Canada. I'm afraid I was fairly rude in answering the question, just as I'm sure Newfoundlanders, if they are indeed capable of being rude, would be if someone asked them about their vision of their own island. The more I continue to get around this country, the more I realize that, whatever it is *Maclean's* magazine and the CIC are now talking about, if you can articulate it, you don't understand it. Show me a man with a pat definition of what makes Canada and I'll show you someone who doesn't know what he's talking about. You can make points about Canada, to be sure — just as you can say of Newfoundland that it is non-plastic, human, vital, exploited, harsh and incredibly lovely — but you have come as short of *defining* it as you would fall short of defining love by saying it's a good healthy roll in the hay.

So these brief reflections are intended to say nothing at all, except that all of us here are still glowing from what we learned in Newfoundland, that we are glowing just as much at the prospects of the places we'll be going next month and after, and that this country in the morning or any *other* time of day is just some place to live, my sons, and there's not a great deal wrong with that.

Peter Gzowski, from *Peter Gzowski's Book About This Country in the Morning*

The District Nurse

Now I'm going to tell you how the District Nurse came to be stationed at Hartley's Harbour instead of here in Pigeon Inlet where she ought to be.

We wanted her here and Hartley's Harbour people were unreasonable enough to want her there. The government couldn't please everybody, so they told her to spend her first three months with us. Then she could decide for herself, and they'd build her dispensary in whatever place she picked.

We in Pigeon Inlet figured out we couldn't lose—for three good reasons. First, a nurse'd want a nice clean store to do her shopping. We had that. Levi Bartle's store in Pigeon Inlet is away ahead of Lige Grimes' old place in Hartley's Harbour. Second, she'd want a good boarding house, and we had that. Aunt Sophy Watkinson's boarding house was famous all along the coast, while in Hartley's Harbour, she'd be lucky if she didn't starve to death at Aunt Sarah Skimple's. Third, and most important of all, she'd probably want some nice company her own age, and that was our strongest point. The Hartley's Harbour boys are all right in their own way, but not to be compared with young Lloyd Walcott, a handsome, strapping young fellow, just like myself thirty years ago. What more could a nurse want?

Well, in November she came down on the boat to Hartley's Harbour and we saw her on the deck of the steamer. Just out from England she was. Pretty little thing, but awful skinny. Anyway, if she didn't starve in the next three months, we'd fatten her up when we got her up in the Inlet in February. We were so sure of getting her now that we began to pick a place to build the dispensary.

We wouldn't have been so sure if we'd known that Lige Grimes had just given up chewing tobacco. He had cleaned up his store and put up a big notice. It read: NO SMOKING OR SPITTING ALLOWED. BY ORDER OF THE HARTLEY'S HARBOUR NURSE'S COMMITTEE. The hypocrite! But we didn't know that 'til 'twas too late.

At last one day in February the nurse moved in by dog team—bag and baggage—to start her three months with us. She looked thinner than ever, but Aunt Sophy was ready with a big supper for her and young Lloyd Walcott dropped in accidentally during the evening.

Our committee had a lot of meetings from then on and Grampa Walcott always had something good to report. Nurse's appetite was good and she was getting fatter every day. She liked Aunt Sophy and young Lloyd was up there every night. Grampa walked in on them in Aunt Sophy's living room one night. He chuckled when he reported this to us and said that courtin' was the one thing that hadn't changed in the last sixty years.

In May the first steamer came and the nurse had to go back to St. John's. She said she'd have to report to the government before deciding where her headquarters would be, but we were sure we had her. Why, she looked a good thirty pounds heavier than she had three months ago. Levi Bartle even bet Lige Grimes a hundred dollars that we'd get her. I don't hold with bettin', especially with fellows like Lige Grimes.

Well, we got our shock a week later, when me and Skipper Joe were sitting down in Levi Bartle's front room listening to the Gerald Doyle news bulletin. The bulletin was about three parts over when we heard this:

"Nurse Plumtree, who is in St. John's on official business, is returning by next boat to take up residence in her new headquarters at Hartley's Harbour."

We looked at each other. There must be some mistake. The bulletin continued: "Nurse Plumtree looks very fit and healthy after her winter in the North. She laughingly admitted to a reporter from this bulletin that she had put on too much weight during the past three months, but that she intended to diet from now on till she had reduced to her normal weight."

We stared in amazement. What was he talking about? The bulletin continued: "Our Hartley's Harbour correspondent informs us that Mr. Lloyd Walcott of Pigeon Inlet has just accepted a position as book-keeper with the enterprising firm of Elijah Grimes of Hartley's Harbour. Mr. Walcott will be taking up his new duties shortly."

I looked at Levi Bartle out of the corner of my eye. His face had turned white as a sheet.

The bulletin continued: "Mr. Grimes has just been awarded the contract to build the new nurse's dispensary in the up and coming town of Hartley's Harbour."

I looked again. Levi's face was turning from white to red—dark red. The reader continued: "The nurse's committee of Hartley's Harbour gratefully acknowledges receipt of a generous donation of one hundred dollars from Mr. Levi Bartle, a popular business man of the little settlement of Pigeon Inlet. This money will be

Beau—Belle

spent by the committee for liquid refreshment at a time to be given in her honour when she arrives shortly to take up her permanent residence in Hartley's Harbour. It is expected that a good time will be had by all."

I looked again. Levi's face was purple now—a deep dark purple. Me and Skipper Joe Irwin tiptoed silently from the room and out through his back door.

You'd think that much of a victory would have satisfied the crowd from Hartley's Harbour. But no! They had to rub it in a bit harder. A few days later, Levi Bartle received something in a big flat envelope and wondered who was sending him a calendar in May. It was postmarked "Hartley's Harbour" and in one corner of the envelope was written: "You can hang this up in *your* store now—*we're* finished with it." Levi opened the envelope and found—yes, you've guessed it. It was a card-board notice showing signs of wear and tear. On it was written in big letters in indelible pencil: NO SMOKING OR SPITTING ALLOWED. BY ORDER OF THE HARTLEY'S HARBOUR NURSE'S COMMITTEE. Poor Levi was fit to be tied.

Well, that'll show you what we Pigeon Inlet people are going to be up against when we try to get a fish plant in Pigeon Inlet instead of in Hartley's Harbour. But we'll do it. Yes, sir! You watch!

from *The Chronicles of Uncle Mose*, by Ted Russell

I'm in love with a clerk
from Trois Rivières
who trills his r's
and slicks his hair;

He's smooth as a seal
his smile is jolly,
though my name is Miriam
he calls me Polly;

He sends me greetings
on golden cards
and mails me snapshots
of snowy yards;

I'm *mauvaise anglaise*—
this he forgives,
between us two
it's live-and-let-lives;
He's in his city,
I'm in mine,
we meet at Easter
on Bleury and Pine;

He calls me Polly,
I call him Patrice,
he says *Madame
a votre service;*

And I say *Monsieur
dis-moi tu,
tu es poupé*
and I love you.

Miriam Waddington

Secretarial Training: '65—'70

My first job
set up by a friend's father
for the "poor kid" fresh outa high school
so confused I got two social insurance numbers
the personnel man alarmed
spoke of jail
i worked
and watched the other women
competing for minor promotions
glancing askance at me
"privileged" at $45 a week
unskilled   temporary
i was scab labour
but there was no union
and none of us then
knew our mistrust of one another
served everybody's interest but our own

    *   *   *

i said to him
(not thinking of myself of course)
   did you know
   she only makes $300 a month
   and has two kids to feed?
he laughed
   i pay more than that in income tax
drove off in his new mercedes
and didn't raise her salary

    *   *   *

he watched me as my pen shook
and dictated faster
she gets off easy enough he thought
sits here reading half the time
   IS IT MY FAULT
   my mind screams
   that business isn't good
   that the company's in trouble
   and the 500 shares you talked me into buying
   at $1.05 (HIGHEST EVER) are now at 15c . . .
   am i supposed to file the same letter 30 times
   dress up and coo for the big wheels
   at $325 a month . . .   ???
    *   *   *
  GET YOUR OWN GODDAMN COFFEE!!!

Shirley Miller

44

Some Day

Some day I'm gonna stand up on my desk
   take all my clothes off
   and hurl the typewriter at your head

   And I'll squirt gestetner ink
   all over your board room
   with its rosewood chairs

Some day I'll shove every paper clip
   into the xerox machine
   and set it at a million

   And then I'll throw your file cabinets
   on your antique carpet
   and piss on them

Some day I'm gonna force you to lick
   1000 envelopes cross-legged
   with nylons on dear

   And I'll make you chew three dozen
   shiny new pencils
   and watch you die of lead poisoning

Someday I'm gonna claim compensation
   for mind rot
   and soul destruction

And for sure I'm never gonna write
one folksy line about the heroism
of women workers

Dierdre Gallagher

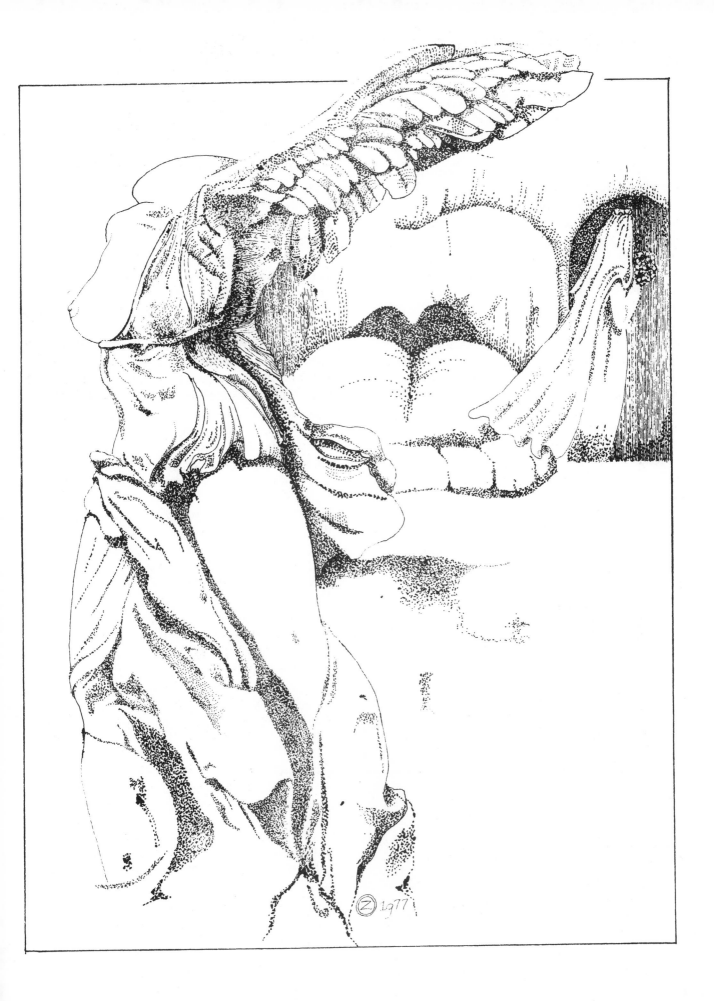

How to make your own paper

1. Make a wooden frame from scrap pieces of wood about six inches by eight inches and about an inch thick.
2. Staple screening tightly and smoothly across the frame. Use nylon screening—it's easier on the fingers and doesn't rust!
3. In a blender mash up an old Christmas or birthday card along with some potato peels, or carrot peels, or any vegetable fibre you happen to have around . . . you'll have to experiment.
4. Dump the mixture (called pulp) into a pail or tub or the kitchen sink filled about four inches deep with water.
5. Grasping your screen in both hands, place it in the tub and shake gently from side to side. Then in a single straight motion lift the screen out of the tub. The water will rush through the screening *but* the fibre will evenly coat it. Try to keep the screen level; if it tips, half your paper will be too thick, and half will be too thin.
6. Now, to get your paper off the screen—which is the tricky part. You will need some old newspapers, laid on a table, and an iron. Hold your screen above the newspaper and turn it over. Mop up the excess water with a sponge; then *very, very* carefully lift up the screen. Your paper will remain on the newspaper. Next put a sheet of newspaper over the new paper and iron it dry so it doesn't tear.

from *The Canadian Inventions Book*, by Janis Nostbakken and Jack Humphrey.

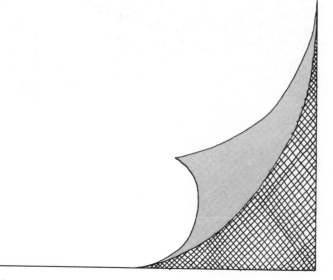

Old Alex

"85 years old, that miserable alcoholic
old bastard is never gonna die," the man said
where he got bed and board. But he did.
I'll say this for Alex' immortality tho:
if they dig him up in a thousand years,
and push a spigot into his belly why
his fierce cackle'll drive a nail in silence,
his laugh split cordwood and trees kow-tow
like green butlers, the staggering world
get drunk and sober men run scared.
So you say: was I fond of him?
No-not exactly anyhow. Once
he told his sons and daughters to bugger off,
and then vomited on their memory. It'd be
like liking toadstools or a gun pointing at you—
He sat home three weeks drinking whiskey,
singing harsh songs and quoting verse and chapter
from the Bible: his mean and privileged piety
dying slowly: theyrolled him onto a stretcher
like an old pig and prettied him with cosmetics,
sucked his blood out with a machine and
dumped him into the ground like garbage.

I don't mourn. Nobody does. Like mourning an ulcer
Why commemorate disease in a poem then?
I don't know. But his hate was lovely,
given freely and without stint. His smallness
had the quality of making everyone else feel noble,
and thus fools. I search desperately
for good qualities, and end up crawling
inside that decaying head and wattled throat
to scream obscenities like papal blessings,
knowing now and again I'm at least God.
Well, who remembers a small purple and yellow
    bruise long?
But when he was here he was a sunset!

Al Purdy

Those trees weren't put on that mountain by God to be praised, they were put there to be chopped down.

Phil Gagliardi
BC cabinet minister

Friends Logging

One day I hear them stomp up the stairs,
kick at my door again, and here they are.
Whether because of the winter shut-down, just a few days off
or because the summertime woods are about to burn
they sit, ask a few questions about my life
and then resume logging: the chainsaws start up, sawdust begins flying,
the air of my room fills with smoke,
the smell of the wet forest, and with the sound
of rigging signals, diesel engines, and the first huge cedar toppling.

"Did you hear the one about the little man
—about so high—who comes into camp and asks for a job as a faller?
'Here's a chainsaw,' they tell him, 'let's see what you can do.
I don't use a saw, he says, *I use this*:
and he holds up a little-bitty axe.
'You can't do anything with that,' they tell him
and he says: *Show me a tree you want cut.*
They do, and in three quick blows
the tree creaks, leans, and crashes down.
'My God,' somebody says, 'where did you learn to fall like that?'
You know the Sahara desert? the little man asks
'Sure.' they reply, 'but there aren't any trees there.'
There aren't now, the little man says."

And that's only speaking with me. If two of them
arrive at the same time, I have to leap under my chair
after less than a minute once they begin to talk to each other
as spruce, hemlock and fir
start dropping to the ground one by one
all over my room. If I go out
for even a few minutes—to get some beer

or something—when I get back
I can hardly push the door open
because of the tangle of branches and roots,
machinery, and the litter of stumps and logs
filling my room like a jumbled windfall.

"There's this chokerman, see, and he saves up enough money
for a trip to Europe. He's flying along in the plane
over Italy, when the pilot comes on the PA
and says the plane has engine trouble
and they are going to issue parachutes so everybody can bail out.
The chokerman begins yelling for his luggage,
he wants his suitcase, right now.
The stewardess tries to calm him down
but he keeps demanding his bag, so finally
they get it for him. He opens his suitcase
and pulls out all he has inside:
a frayed, kinked, twisted, horrible-looking cable.
'What use is that?' asks the stewardess.
'The plane is going to crash. You need a parachute.'
Not me, says the chokerman. *This damn cable
will hang up anywhere.*"

Even they admit it is sometimes too much.
Everyone talks about the job after work,
but who else but these speak about it night and day?
Steve tells me: "I'm lying asleep, first night back in Vancouver,
when a train goes by and blows its whistle: *hoot*, hoot hoot.
Now that's a logging signal
so I start to dream I'm standing in the wrong place

and this gigantic log is bearing down on me . . . "

And Mark: "We're sitting in the pub talking
about the number of logs we've yarded that day
and about the most anyone has ever yarded that we've heard of.
One of the guys who drives a caterpillar tractor
meanwhile is trying to squeeze past us to get to the can
but nobody is paying much attention
Finally he says in a loud voice:
Do you mind moving your cold deck
so I can get my cat through?"
On and on: while the waiter re-fills the table,
the hills get barer and barer
and my words spill across their paper, into the common air.

Tom Wayman

Seymour Inlet Float Camp:
Domestic Scene

mother is sewing
father's
thumb back on

John Marshall

Canadian Railroad Trilogy

There was a time in this fair land when the railroad did not run,
When the wild majestic mountains stood alone against the sun,
Long before the white man and long before the wheel
When the green dark forest was too silent to be real.

But time has no beginnings and history has no bounds,
As to this verdant country they came from all around,
They sailed upon her waterways and they walked the forests tall,
Built the mines, the mills and the factories for the good of us all.

And when the young man's fancy was turnin' in the spring,
The railroad men grew restless for to hear the hammers ring,
Their minds were overflowin' with the visions of their day
And many a fortune won and lost and many a debt to pay.

For they looked in the future and what did they see,
They saw an iron road runnin' from the sea to the sea,
Bringin' the goods to a young, growin' land
All up from the seaports and into their hands.
"Look away!", said they, "across this mighty land,
From the eastern shore to the western strand!"

"Bring in the workers and bring up the rails,
We gotta lay down the tracks and tear up the trails,
Open her heart, let the life blood flow,
Gotta get on our way 'cause we're movin' too slow
Get on our way 'cause we're movin' too slow."

"Behind the blue rockies the sun is declinin',
The stars they come stealin' at the close of the day,
Across the wide prairie our loved ones lie sleeping
Beyond the dark ocean in a place far away."

"We are the navvies who work upon the railway,
Swingin' our hammers in the bright blazin' sun,
Livin' on stew and drinkin' bad whiskey,
Bendin' our backs 'til the long days are done."

"We are the navvies who work upon the railway,
Swingin' our hammers in the bright blazin' sun,
Layin' down track and buildin' the bridges,
Bendin' our backs 'til the railroad is done."

"So over the mountains and over the plains,
Into the muskeg and into the rain,
Up the Saint Lawrence all the way to Gaspé,
Swingin' our hammers and drawin' our pay,
Layin' 'em in and tyin' 'em down,
Away to the bunkhouse and into the town,
A dollar a day and a place for my head
A drink to the living, a toast to the dead!"

"Oh, the song of the future has been sung,
All the battles have been won,
On the mountain tops we stand,
All the world at our command.
We have opened up the soil
With our teardrops—
And our toil."

For there was a time in this fair land when the railroad did not run,
When the wild majestic mountains stood alone against the sun,
Long before the white man and long before the wheel,
When the green dark forest was too silent to be real
When the green dark forest was too silent to be real.
And many are the dead men,
Too silent
To be real.

Gordon Lightfoot

Station for a Sentimental Journey

I know that Union Station is a cold, stony, hollow, and dreary institution but, all the same, I have a profound affection for the place. I can't even walk past those grim pillars and that long cliff of drab old stone without having this faint stir of anticipation move within me, without remembering that Union Station, the muggy smell of the place, is an unshakable connection with whatever decisions I've made to influence my future.

It was from Union Station that I took the first train of my life, a very long and unspeakably thrilling one that crept north for six hours to a cottage beyond Huntsville. It was from there that I left, going away to a farm in Nova Scotia . . .

going away to my first real job, as a reporter in Ottawa . . . going away, I once thought, for ever.

And it was to Union Station that I returned . . . coming home, flat broke, to get married . . . coming home, flat broke, from England . . . coming home, flat broke, from California . . . in and out, in and out of Union Station at strange times of the day and night . . . under the stone walls that are massive, but never so massive they don't shake with the rumbling by of passing trains . . . down there where the artificial light seems always to speak of winter afternoons, and there's always a nun in the waiting-room,

Each May, I'd come back from university in

New Brunswick and, because spring arrives a little late there, the ride to Ontario was like speeding into summer. The moment I stepped into Union Station, I'd smell the new heat, the lake, the water in the leaves of Toronto, the size of the city, and the potential of the months to come.

And, on this particular Saturday afternoon, I happen to be pushing some papers around in my downtown office and I should really go over to the post office anyway, so I begin to drift over toward the old station to watch other people move between the places in their lives.

I start at the corner of Wellington and Yonge and pass the Variety Centre. Its window is crammed with deodorants, gold-plated pillboxes, pistol cigarette-lighters, little plastic bugs that creep out of a glassful of beer or across your pant-leg to provide "no end of fun for the whole family", and transistor radios that look like whisky bottles, golf clubs, rubber tires, globes, even midget television sets.

Then I walk west on the north side of Front and, for at least the thirtieth time, find myself sidetracked by the Old Favourites Book Shop.

This time, I invest two dollars in *All About Canada for Little Folk*. It's a Grade 1 reader, written in 1924 by one W.J. Dickie, and includes photographs and stories about the royal family: 'This is the Prince of Wales on his pony. His name is Edward. He is the oldest son of the King and Queen. He will be King someday. He is a jolly Prince. He is always smiling. He came to Canada to visit. We were very glad to see him. The people made many parties for him. He had a good time."

But, onward to Union Station. I perform my postal duties, and walk west—past the spot where a bronze plaque advises me that "at this place, on May 16, 1853, the first train in Ontario, hauled by a steam locomotive, started and ran to Aurora"—and on into that great lobby; that humming, sleepy cave, where the travellers are always nervous or sorrowful or excited, the railroad employees are maddeningly casual, and the ceiling is so astonishingly high in the useless space that I can never look up there without remembering, for a flash, how it felt to be three-and-a-half feet high.

Downstairs—in the low, grey place where thousands upon thousands of immigrants have welcomed thousands upon thousands of newer immigrants, and clutched them and cried and laughed and hollered and reeled around with them—there is very little action today.

There are only a few teen-age boys down there. Some of them are making what they take to be screamingly funny faces in the booth where, for twenty-five cents, you can get four pictures of yourself. A few others are over in the Amuse-O-Matic Centre, shooting gangsters with the Riot Gun, shooting monsters with the Monster Gun, shooting rustlers with the Texas Ranger Gatling Gun, or investigating a peep show.

One of the peep shows is so old the instructions are no longer legible and, when you drop your nickel in and start cranking the brass handle and the dog-eared photos begin to flutter past, you see three pretty girls and they're dancing around in a circle with their hands joined. Their blossomy petticoats flop around heavily and the big moment comes when, together, they do cartwheels. There is something pastoral and absurdly innocent about the whole scene. Today, I guess, the girls are as old as Charlie Chaplin.

It is mid afternoon now, and I can feel the Montreal train coming into the station. I wait to see who'll come down from the platform and along this historic pavilion that leads to the city. I give the weight machine a dime and it tells me that not only do I weigh 166 pounds but that, since this is December and my sign of the zodiac is Cancer, "Your bad humor and temper, especially in the morning, is due to your poor health. Remember, if you want to sell yourself, you have got to do it with a smile. Your sentimental life is at a minimum."

Now, a few old ladies with paper bags are walking down toward the taxi stand, and a blond kid of about eighteen heads straight for the phone booths. He's got a huge knapsack strapped to his back, along with a pair of football pants and a guitar. He sets all the stuff down, finds a dime, picks up the guitar, climbs into a booth, phones somebody, and starts strumming away to the receiver. I calculate he is not a Cancerian; his sentimental life is obviously at a maximum.

from *The Short Happy Walks of Max MacPherson*, by Harry Bruce

Train Song

This is a train song
It's a song about gettin' lost
It's a song about what that cost
This is a train song
For birds that are stuck on the ground
For ears that only listen
For distant sounds.

Hear the mourning of the midnight whistle
Hear the ringin' of the railroad sign
On the double steel high line
They say every railroad line has a bad side
Where they make all the poor people stay
Though some of the bad ones
Might make it across
That train passes by anyway.

This is a train song
It's a song about gettin' lost
It's a song about what that cost
This is a train song
For birds that are stuck on the ground
For ears that only listen
For distant sounds.

Murray McLauchlan, from his record *On the Boulevard*.

I saw the sky fill up with engine
Heard the world fill up with noise
Laid a penny on the track, got a flapjack back
As the driver waved to the boys
I watched the people at the window
From the bushes as the diner flew by
Now I look from the window of the diner
For a kid with hungry eyes.

This is a train song
It's a song about gettin' lost
It's a song about what that cost
This is a train song
For birds that are stuck on the ground
For ears that only listen
For distant sounds.

Just me and the stars on a flatcar
As the train pulled into Schreiber town
Cop saw me jump and I was runnin'
I was scared he's gonna run me down
Now I see the porter smilin' to my left hand
As he's lookin' at the money
That I'm holdin' in my right
And I think how it's nice he wants to know
   my name
And I laugh out the window at the night

Riding on the Ocean Limited:
or, Otto, Spare That Train!

The morning is full of sunlit, sterling-silver mist and the cold fragrance of a clean day by the sea. I board the train with the great name—the Ocean Limited—and, the moment she starts to glide into her long flight from salt water, I remember a song. It's a fine, rushing pop song in which Americans celebrate a train called The City of New Orleans, and I wish we had one like it. If ever a train deserved a song, it's The Ocean Limited. We'll be gone 500 miles when day is done.

My last sight of Halifax harbour includes a graceful black vessel called the Gulf Star. And now, in a deep gorge of dark stone, the Ocean Limited picks up speed and plunges through my own neighbourhood. Creak, groan. Clackety-clack. Rumble, rumble. Ah, there's my sailboat tugging at her mooring in the Northwest Arm. Gone already. We explode on Bedford Basin and, as the train bends around the shore, I can see her zebra-striped engine with the orange snout as she ships us all onward, ever onward, through sunshine and shadow, and into the life of the country. Long before lunch, the distant bridges over Halifax harbour disappear astern.

It is children's day in the sticks. People in airplanes will never know. The summer is young, the buds in the trees are as fine as lace, as light as a breath of pale, green smoke and, at the edge of every glittering stream we thunder past, there's a clutch of kids with fishing poles. . . . Two boys on a raft sword-fight with branches. . . . Seven more play touch football. Their audience is a black, tethered pony. . . . A gang plays ferocious ball hockey within thirty feet of the track. . . . A thin little girl rambles along a dirt road with a bag of milk. She's in no hurry. She practises twitching her hips like a bigger girl. . . . A tiny boy in maroon pants cartwheels across his lawn, past the garden swings, past the retired snowmobile, past the turning leaves, past my flying window forever. Two girls rise up in the back of a parked truck, wave all four arms and throw huge smiles to salute once more the ancient glory of the Ocean Limited. . . .

Men join one another to shingle roofs, play golf, fix car engines, paddle canoes, plough fields the color of chocolate fudge. . . . Women rake leaves, tend gardens, wash windows, hang out triumphant streams of windblown laundry, pause among apple blossoms to consider our whistling charge into the dark, northern woods, over the bottomless bogs of New Brunswick and, after

nightfall, on into the craggy Alpine gullies and mysterious towns of one of the least-known stretches of Quebec. The hotel signs blink red and green up here. There's a card game in an old house with a mansard roof on the bank of the Matapedia River. It's gone. And there goes a house party, a woman dancing in her living room, windows that show no light at all except the secret, blue glow of television. . . .

Wherever we stop, the platform swims with the comings and goings of Canadian lives, the smiles of greeting, the tears of parting. Hello. Goodbye. God bless. Write soon. Be good now. And in the bar-car, I chat with a man who lived where I did in 1957, on the banks of the Gatineau River near Ottawa, a man who has never forgotten the redness of Gatineau maples in October. I meet a woman whose brother, it turns out, was a classmate of mine in Sackville, New Brunswick more than twenty years ago. An old lady says her grandson, a brakeman, desperately wants to become an engineer, so he can actually drive the trains. I tell her I can understand that; it's hard to mind your own business aboard the Ocean Limited.

And twenty-two hours out of Halifax, on a morning of heat and beauty, the train springs me right into the bright and breezy heart of Montreal; and please, Otto Lang, whatever you do to increase the economic efficiency of rail travel, spare the Ocean Limited. She's not just a train. She's part of my Canadian soul.

Harry Bruce

Our Motto Was, "Drive 'er Till She Quits...

I think now that, instead of getting $395 for The Heap against the price of another car, I should have sold her to a museum. For she was a classic. She was the archetypal North American Family Car of the first half of the eighth decade of the 20th century. The Heap was quintessentially ordinary. God, what a *boring* car! Other drivers scarcely saw her in parking lots, smacked her without malice, disappeared without guilt. Dents and scratches competed with rust patches and bird crap to make The Heap's naturally dull complexion even less attractive than it would otherwise have been. Her colour was faded turquoise, pockmarked.

Her name was pedestrian. This was no Malibu, Parisienne, Capri, Granada, Thunderbird, Galaxie, Fury Toronado or Gran Torino. No sir, The Heap was a 1970 Pontiac Stratochief, and every inch a wallflower. She had six cylinders, four doors, an automatic gearshift, a radio and an ashtray that, under moderate pressure, dumped butts, apple cores and gum wrappers on your ankles. The stuff under the backseat cushion was only slightly more intriguing: matchbox cars, dried-out ballpoint pens, eyebrow pencils, Smarties and cookie crumbs, straws, paper clips, subscription cards out of 1972 magazines, tickets on dead lotteries.

The Heap's interior was hearse-black. Wherever we went—and she took us 88,343 miles—we fought an atmosphere of deep mourning. Sometimes the mourning was for whatever it was we'd put in the trunk, which let in water even faster than the engine let out oil. She was a big car but, on highway hills, less than peppy. Few driving experiences are more humiliating than having an Austin Mini overtake you, honk you aside, then hurtle over the horizon ahead.

Then Get a Tow Truck..."

She had a lifelong weakness, an Achilles' heel, an Orr's knee. Where the exhaust pipe joined the engine manifold, there was something called a doughnut gasket. The gasket burned out every few thousand miles and the results were, first, that The Heap sounded as though she had no muffler and, second, that exhaust fumes flowed inside and nauseated children who were already woozy. Yes, the all-time Family Car. But as she roared slowly down the highway, with the radio squawking, the windows open to release fumes and the kids puking into plastic garbage bags, we looked more like a gang of boozing, teenaged goons than the respectable, downwardly mobile family we really were.

We are not car people. We don't even fasten our seat belts. Our motto was, "Drive 'er till she quits. Then get a tow truck." We let her tires get soft,

her filters clog, her oil get dirty, her wires rot, her timing deteriorate, her exhaust pollute the neighbourhood, her backfiring sound like a shootout at a bank robbery. If a door handle broke, we left it broken. There were three other doors, weren't there? We never washed her, waxed her, repaired dents. We failed to get our safety checks on time and, if The Heap had been a horse, animal lovers would have had me in court years ago. Yet, she was just what the used-car ads promise when they're flogging wrecks: "Good transportation."

She took us farther than three-and-half-times around the world. She helped us move out of three houses and into two. She was older than the cat, and our children can scarcely remember life without The Heap. She brought them to Nova Scotia. In times that cannot ever come back, in

some of the best seasons of our life together, she
carried us off to the sweetest shores on earth. As
the used-car salesman cast a cold eye on her, I
thought, I really can't stand cars but, if he says
one contemptuous word about The Heap, I'll take
my business elsewhere. No lady should have to
endure insults from strangers.

Harry Bruce

Grease is Cheaper Than Parts

That old truck's got a lot of heart,
Remember that grease is cheaper than parts;
Rather change your oil than your piston rings,
Listen to the motor, hear old Harvey sing.

Now I called up old Harvey one morning
Just to pass the time of day,
And his true wife said with a tear in her eye,
"Old Harvey's passed away."
So I went and took that beat-up truck
To the hill where the old man lies;
Now Harvey can run that Econoline van
Down the 401 in the sky.
Singin':
That old truck's got a lot of heart,
Remember that grease is cheaper than parts;
Rather change your oil than your piston rings,
Listen to the motor, hear old Harvey sing.

That old mechanic had a lot of heart,
He taught me that grease is cheaper than parts;
Rather change your oil than your piston rings,
Listen to the motor, hear old Harvey sing.

Dave Essig, from his record, *Stewart Crossing*

A '63 Ford Econoline van,
It seemed like a home to me.
It ran and it ran 'til it busted a cam
With a case of engine fatigue.
Old Harvey came out with his pick-up truck
In the middle of a driving rain,
And he towed her home and he fixed her up,
And it ran real good again,
Singin':
That old truck's got a lot of heart,
Remember that grease is cheaper than parts;
Rather change your oil than your piston rings,
Listen to the motor, hear old Harvey sing.

Harvey was kind of a crazy old man,
But he was never nobody's fool.
I'd stand around and help him the best I could
Pass a wrench and slip him a tool.
He'd crank on this and he'd crank on that,
And he'd curse and swear till she'd run.
Now it's many years later as I look back,
And it was always a lot of fun.
Singin':

The Education of a Class A Mechanic

Peter always could catch or throw a ball with either hand. And at twelve he could kill pigeons on the wing with a bow. He preferred to fish for them, though, with Barry Staples. Barry was a hired hand, and small for sixteen.

They'd climb up to the top of the corn silo with a fish net. Peter would hang onto the rungs on the outside, and Barry would edge along the outside of the silo. The reason their method worked is that a scared pigeon will always fly upwards. So when Peter was ready at the triangular opening in the silo roof, net in hand, Barry would pound on the metal roof. A pigeon would burst up flapping through the opening, and Peter would swipe at it. They got $5 live, $2 dead from an Italian who came out from the city. That kept them in pocket money all one summer.

Peter always had jobs, worked hard and got along. When he was five, he had to be put to bed for two days from overwork. An uncle had jokingly told him to "shovel out that horse stall."

But work was never his equal. I mean, work is subordinate to him, not the other way round. When I have to move, I'd rather do it with Peter. So would the other kids in the family. We tend to fret and worry and get tense. But with Peter, if a chest of drawers slides down a flight of stairs, you laugh.

His attitude to school was the same. He didn't think his measure was to be taken by marks or by what the teachers thought of him. I was oldest, so I helped the others. I passed Grade 9 French three times. With Peter, it was fun: "If you hear her say "ett voo", you say "Juh swee". Peter: "Hah! Juh swee. Some system."

Peter stayed at my house this fall while he was taking courses at a community college, and I was fascinated by the ease with which he studied. I've seen graduate students approach studying like an old dog making its nest for the night. They turn round and round until they get *down*. Peter didn't even sharpen pencils. He just borrowed a scribbler, and reviewed his notes each night. When something wasn't immediately clear from the text, he'd ask an instructor the next day. He was attending courses towards his auto mechanic's license. Maybe it was easier for him to study because the content of the courses was so familiar to him. We grew up on a highly mechanized farm, with a machine shop to carry out repairs on the tractors, combines, spreaders, etc., Peter used both the arc and the oxy-acetylene

welders there, and took shop courses in high school. I don't think it was just this experience that got him top marks in welding this fall on his course. He has a knack for it. He has this comfortable relationship with the physical world. He understands its logic.

When our parents moved to Bowmanville from the farm, Peter's social life changed. It began to revolve around cars, like most of the kids' in the area. In fact, when an area is so dominated by one industry as the Oshawa area is by General Motors, even the sub-cultures are car-oriented. A group known as the Bowmanville Beach Boys live by the lake in winterized homes. They paint the undersides of their cars fluorescent orange and jack up the rear ends on big wheels. (Like breaking a horse's tail and resetting it.) Peter doesn't associate with them. "They're pretty extreme." If you drive by one of their houses, they look at you suspiciously from around their cars like accolytes at a shrine. As Peter says "They're a little out of it." But there's common ground. All the kids in the area go on tours. Tours are a way of mocking, of transcending how little there is to do. You take a tour—and you don't pay attention to where you are or where you're going. You might end up in Lakefield before a night's tour is through. (I think my Dad used to do this. I think it was called "back roadin'".) They roll down the windows, turn up Max Webster on the tape deck, drink, joke, make love, push the car back out of the ditch, smoke and laugh. The younger ones drag on the Taunton Road.

Peter loves it. He's good at it. The milieu fits him.

He's worked at gas stations since he's been old enough, with the exception of one summer as cook's helper on a road crew. (There were a lot of small potatoes pitched into the bush that summer.) The year before he started his apprenticeship, he managed a gas station by himself. Enterprise Hollow, at the intersection of 116 and 35. He organized the books, planted petunias, and painted the overhead door. Said Quebeckers were the best customers because they tipped. For a short time he worked on the assembly line at G.M. Unlike most of the other young people who start there, Peter didn't go back after his first lay-off. There aren't very many escapes from the bell curve especially if you don't have an aptitude for academics. But for someone like Peter, a trade can give you some independence. He has to work long

hours as an apprentice. At work at 8, and stay 'til 7. An hour for lunch. Six days a week. The government subsidizes part of his wages. His boss, Mike Koll, is only a few years older than Peter, and owns a garage in Hampton. Hampton's pretty. It has a tree-lined main street, and the shop window looks out onto river cedars choke thick with wild vine. Mike sets a high standard for Greenaway's Garage. He got his papers after a straight five years. He just went and wrote his final exam after that time. Most kids get some hours taken off their apprenticeship according to the number of years of high school they have.

In one day, Peter might organize the tow calls, weld a kid's snowmobile ski, advise a farmer on the right weight of diesel fuel for his tractor and work on an engine. A friend or two might drop by for some help or advice. When they talk about a problem, social intonations in their speech fall by the wayside. They are engaged in a relationship with a body of knowledge, and the conversations are sincere and soberly conducted. Not unlike, one imagines, a doctor's conference. Mechanics build up a loyal clientele the way a doctor does. People come in ignorance and trust, relying on their specialized skills and knowledge. But auto mechanics is one of the few jobs open to those without middle class skills that offers some independence. And there is no profession more hated, it seems, by the middle class. "They don't write exposés about doctors in the *Star*," said Peter wryly. "You know, some guy goes around with a sore big toe, and then writes up how long he waited in the doctor's office, and what

explanation the doctor offered, and how much he was charged. But they do it to the mechanics every year. Some places charge too much, but the mechanic doesn't get that, the management does. It's not often a guy in business by himself will rip you off."

Peter doesn't like working under anyone, and he says he doesn't like the idea of someone working under him. He'd like to own a garage with a partner and divide up the work. Either that or, after he did so well on his courses, he began considering another possibility. One of the teachers, the one in charge of the tune up section of the course, told Peter that two summers at OCE would qualify him after he gets his licence to teach in a high school or community college. I asked Peter if he didn't think there'd be

disadvantages to that. He said, "Yeah. The staff meetings. Heh, heh."

In the meantime though, Peter's back at Greenaway's. His girlfriend in Hampton is no doubt glad that the two month course is over. And his boss must have been glad to see him back. Peter asked him for a raise, and Mike asked him if he could "give a guy a break". Peter: "No, I don't think I can. It's coming to me, and I don't think I can afford not to get it." Mike grumbled a bit, and went off. Then he came back. Mike: "Well, I guess it's okay. I think you're worth it."

By next September, Peter will have completed his hours and then he goes on course again for two months. At the end, he'll be a Class A mechanic. At least.

Helen Sutherland

My '48 Pontiac

All winter long it wouldn't start
standing in the yard covered with snow
I'd go out at 10 below zero and coax
and say
            "Where's your pride?"
and kick it disgustedly
Finally snow covered everything
but television aerials and the world was
a place nobody came to
so white it couldn't be looked at
before nothing was something
But the old Pontiac lay there
affirming its identity
like some prehistoric vegetarian
stupidly unaware of snow
waiting for Tyrannosaurus Rex
to come along and bite off its fenders
"You no good American Pontiac you
(I'd say)
you're a disgrace to General Motors"
then go out and hitch up the dog team.
When June hurried by it still wouldn't start
only stop
and the wreckers hauled it away

Now and then I go to visit my old friend
at Bud's Auto Wreckers
being sentimental about rubber and metal
I think it's glad to see me
and wags both tail lights
a true heart thumping eagerly
under the torn seat covers
I sit behind the wheel
on a parched August afternoon
and we drive thru a glitter of broken glass
among suicides and automotive murders
mangled chryslers and volkswagens
metal twisted into a look
of fierce helplessness
reversed violence in hunchback shapes
and containing it still
waiting to explode outward
when some jolly unlicensed mechanic
(finally identified as pappa sahib)
limps downstairs to give the signal

We drive between dismantled buicks and
studebakers and one stuckup old cadillac
driven to Bud's by a doddering old chauffeur
who used to play poker with Roman chariot
    drivers
and a silent crumpled grey plymouth
with bloodstains on the instrument panel
where a girl died
a '41 de soto with all the chrome gone
still excited from drag races
and quivering blondes whose bottoms it liked
My last visit was by moonlight and flashlight
to Bud's Auto Wreckers
where the old Pontiac waited

I turned the speedometer back to 5000 miles
changed the oil
polished the headlights to look at death
adjusted the rear view mirror to look at life
gave it back its ownership card
and went away
puzzled by things.

    Al Purdy

Editor's Note: The car in the photograph is an authentic
'48 Pontiac. However, as far as we know, the man is not
Al Purdy.

Silver Wheels

high speed drift on a prairie road
hot tires sing like a string being bowed
sudden town rears up then explodes
fragments resolve into white line code
whirl on silver wheels

black earth energy receptor fields
undulate under a grey cloud shield
we outrun a river colour brick red mud
that cleaves apart hills soil rich as blood
whirl on silver wheels

highway squeeze in construction steam
stop caution hard hat yellow insect machines
silver steel towers stalk rolling land
toward distant stacks that shout "Feed on demand"
whirl on silver wheels
whirl on silver wheels

100 miles later the sky has changed
urban anticipation—we get four lanes
redorange furnace sphere notches down
throws up silhouette skyline in brown
whirl on silver wheels

sundogs flare on windshield glass
sudden swoop skyward iron horse overpass
pass a man walking like the man in the moon
walking like his head's full of Irish fiddle tunes
whirl on silver wheels

the skin around every city looks the same
miles of flat neon spelling well-known names
USED TRUCKS DIRTY DONUTS YOU YOU'RE THE ONE
fat wheeled cars squeal into the sun
whirl on silver wheels

radio speakers gargle top forty trash
muzak sound truck to slow collapse
planet engines pulsate in sidereal time
if you listen close you can hear the whine
whirl on silver wheels
whirl on silver wheels.

Bruce Cockburn, from his record, *In the Falling
Dark*.

The Ballad of the Red Dumptruck

I'd like to live in Vancouver, West Coast sunny shore
But there is something here in Musgrave that I like even more;
And the thing that I might get, and all I need is a little luck
Is to sit behind the wheel of the Council's red dumptruck.
How nice to be in that big GM
The motor with power to spare
And the new ones won't be out
For at least another year.
You take a load of gravel
To be spread over the hill
You just sit there smiling
Looking through the big windshield.
That great big dump there on the rear
Is a thousand pounds or more
Them great big double headlights and
The split shift on the floor.
The clearance lights and safety glass . . . a man must feel so free
Blowing for the open road in the Council's GMC
The man who's got a job on it, he's got to take a test.
Beaton Abbot's got the contract to keep the tires the very best.
The rubber must be perfect
So it won't get stumped
Because there are no rebuilt parts
For the Council's red dumptruck.
Bill Whiteway is the driver, he's been driving it a year
Oh how happy I'll be when he quits his job
And goes back to Bay de Spear.
But it's only then I'll get the chance
To really change my luck
And to sit behind the wheel
Of the Council's red dumptruck.

Andy Mouland when he was in Grade 11, Musgrave Harbour, Newfoundland

Riverdale Lion

Bound lion, almost blind from meeting their gaze and popcorn,
   the Saturday kids love you. It is their parents
who would paint your mane with polkadots to match
   their California shirts
and would trim your nails for tieclips.

Your few roars delight them. But they wish you would
   quicken your pace
and not disappear so often into your artificial cave
for there they think you partake of secret joys and race
through the jungle-green lair of memory
under an African sun as gold as your mane.

But you fool them. You merely suffer the heat and scatter the flies
with your tail. You never saw Africa.
The sign does not tell them that you were born here, in captivity,
that you are as much a Canadian as they are.

John Robert Colombo

Ten Elephants on Yonge Street

Just about everything
or everyone
has passed up or down:

William Lyon Mackenzie's boys
on the quick way down
from Montgomery's Tavern,
Year of Tyrants
1837.

Wendell Willkie smiling
his 1940 smile
with planes overhead
and the crowds gone crazy,
the year he could have made
Prime Minister!

But until today
never elephants.
Ten gray eminences moving
with the daintiest of steps
and the greatest unconcern
up the canyon.
                  Too bored to yawn
or toss the fools riding them,
they slowly twist their trunks
and empty their bowels
at a pace which keeps
the two men following
with shovels and hand-cart
almost swearingly busy.

Raymond Souster

ROAD FORKS AND GREASY SPOONS

One of those moments in life, which return not because they are wonderful but because they are unavoidable, is the moment when I am sitting at the steering wheel of my truck somewhere on the Trans-Canada highway, and hunger strikes. What I used to do was stop at a big glossy gas station and eat a cheeseburger. At first it seemed amusing and in the holiday spirit to indulge in the prefrozen, prepackaged mixture of grain, preservatives and ground hooves that passes for food at these identical feeding stops where cars

funnel off the road on their way to the trough. But it was bad for me.

This spring, when I was preparing to leave Edmonton after a stint as writer-in-residence at the University of Alberta, I pulled out the old road map. It was supplied by one of the gas companies, and from the locations of their restaurants little red stars sparkled happily. My stomach sent a few warning cramps.

And so I decided to try something different. I would go into all those strange little places that the standardized gas station restaurants are

supposed to liberate us from. Places that belong only to the spot where they stand, corner stores on the national road. Places where real people go regularly, and where they serve real food. Not only would this be kind to my stomach, but it could give me something to think about other than the white line. I did not divulge my plan to my passenger, a fellow refugee from Edmonton who had taken on the name of Geoffrey Hamburg.

Day One

Lunch. We stopped at Helen's Cafe in Innisfree, an attractive town of 300 people sixty miles east of Edmonton on the Yellowhead Highway. It is easy to find in the midst of rolling Ukrainian farm country dotted with prosperous looking barns and shiny-domed churches. Helen's Cafe doubles as the Greyhound bus depot and seemed especially promising because the owner dared put her name on the sign.

It's a low wooden building with white walls, orange curtains, and white wooden booths that resemble roofless dog houses. At lunch time Helen's was crowded—besides a few fellow tourists there were school children, townspeople and farmers. It seemed to be a gathering place as much as a restaurant; conversations wound among the booths and tables as if they had being going on for years.

The atmosphere was vigorous and friendly. Helen herself is a grey-haired woman of indeterminate age who can cook, waitress, tally the bills and talk, all at once. She couldn't convince me to order cabbage rolls so she told me they came with my hot turkey sandwich—as the vegetable. Hamburg, who is a vegetarian, ordered pierogis—boiled dough with a variety of possible fillings. On this day sauerkraut, cheddar cheese, and mashed potatoes were being used. At six for ninety cents they seemed a bargain.

While waiting I inspected the décor: plastic

flowers, ads for Copenhagen Chewing Tobacco, and the world's largest multicoloured jawbreakers were featured. On the walls were extremely odd seascapes painted by Helen's husband. The borscht came.

"Hamburg," I confessed, "I have to tell you something. This trip is being recorded for posterity. I am the Charles Darwin of strange restaurants and you are to be my invaluable assistant. From now on it is your duty to rate everything you eat on a one to ten scale."

"Six," he said, meaning the borscht. "It's got peas and carrots in it."

At first Hamburg seemed happy about the ratings and I trusted him. Later he became evasive and would eventually rate the waitress, but not the food. Meanwhile I quibbled.

"My grandmother puts peas in her borscht," I said.

"Six," he insisted. I myself would have given it a seven. It was lukewarm and thin, but a perfect colour—fluorescent flamingo.

When the pierogis came, Hamburg looked at them suspiciously. Foreign food. They lay on his plate—white, moist, helpless. He touched them with his fork. The skin yielded, then broke open in a hiss of steam.

"These look strange." I told him he needed sour cream. He ladled it on. "Eight," he said. A very high mark from him. The hot turkey sandwich was good but not compelling. But the cabbage rolls were great: ten out of ten.

The coffee was good, too. Though Helen's was crowded and busy, we didn't feel rushed. In fact the whole effect was very relaxing, like eating in someone's kitchen.

And everyone seemed to be getting what he wanted at Helen's—except perhaps Helen herself. As I drank my coffee I overheard her saying that the ambition of her life was to own a Chinese restaurant.

Dinner. As the sun sank hungrily into the horizon, Hamburg and I began to discuss the next meal. Helen's had made us hopeful. "Let's get right off the highway this time," Hamburg said. "We need some local colour."

The sky was pink when we saw the sign: Yellowhead Hotel. A big arrow pointed south of the highway. We followed it into a town called Elstow. In the faded light it looked like a movie set from a western that had been made forty years ago. Dusty wooden buildings, wide streets, windows masking white curtains. Behind the deserted railyards we found the hotel—a brown insulbrick building with paint peeling off the doors and glassless windows. Inside, the first thing I saw was a small mountain of empty Pepsi Cola cases. To the right of the mountain was a beverage room. There was only one customer and he was sipping slowly at a glass of beer. Presently a woman appeared.

"I was looking for the dining room," I said.

"Well, this ain't it."

I looked around. She was absolutely right. There was nothing here but the leftovers of a Pepsi orgy.

"It's up the highway now," she said. She pointed at the door.

You'll see the sign. Yellowhead Hotel. Don't go.

But don't drive right through Elstow either, because the Esso station there has the world's best hot turkey sandwiches. Brown bread, good gravy, lots of meat. The green beans came out of a can and were awful, but the pan fries were just right.

Even Hamburg was satisfied with his fried egg sandwich. He was so happy he ordered raisin pie: a nine. We left happy.

Day Two

Breakfast. Saturday night in Wynyard, Saskatchewan, had been memorable for the locals who came to drink in the tavern of our motel and have drag races in the parking lot. All night I dreamed of inventing the perfect muffler. In the morning I walked down the main street until I came to the only restaurant I was able to see—The Capri Chinese and Canadian Food. The sight of a Chinese restaurant in the middle of the Saskatchewan prairie seemed somehow reassuring. I went inside. The furnishings were perfectly familiar from Chinese restaurants everywhere: a long counter, red booths, juke boxes, elaborate plastic menus.

A man I thought was a customer got up from his seat and brought me a coffee. And before I could even taste it the cook came out from the kitchen and took my order for scrambled eggs. I sipped at the coffee: an esoteric mixture of bleach and soap. When the eggs came, they had been cooked in so much grease that they glowed bright yellow. In color they seemed to be a cousin to Helen's borscht. In taste they were unique. The customer must have been a paid impostor. After a tactful pause I buried the remaining egg under the toast and went outside to stand in the sun.

My eyes were now working well enough to see that there was another restaurant in Wynyard, Saskatchewan—the 7-Up Cafe—just across the street. Hamburg came walking out of it, looking happy.

"Tell me it was awful."

"It was wonderful," he said. "The waitress burned her hand buttering the toast as soon as it came up. She let me substitute milk for coffee on the special. The eggs were like clouds." Three stars.

Lunch. Just after noon we came to the Assiniboine Valley. It is announced by a sudden and beautiful break in the prairie, erupting in hills and deep slashes with bright green grass and horses grazing. This is near Russell, Manitoba, and though we never found the town, we soon found a big, low-slung grey building that looked new and was lined outside with expensive cars. We pulled in, deciding to check out this obvious touch of class.

In the lobby there was glass and deep red carpet. Past it was a beverage room with twenty drinkers all at one long happy table, a fancy dining lounge and a kitchen where I found myself looking in on the baking of fresh rolls. It looked promising.

We chose the cafeteria. Like every other restaurant on the prairies it had orange curtains. Also, it had Muzak. Everything was brand new and there was a cop sitting at the next table. If it hadn't been for the highway going by I would have thought I was in a giant all-night drugstore. I read on the back of the menu that Russell's economy is mainly agricultural, and that this new motel-restaurant, caters to special functions and conventions. There were a lot of happy-looking senior citizens wandering the halls.

Hamburg had searched the menu for meatless

luncheons: pierogis were the choice again. I ordered Napoleon Soup because I had to find out what it was. It was green pepper, tricornered noodles, parsley and carrots—all in a beef base. I gave it an eight. On the other hand, Hamburg's pierogis looked revolting, all white and yellow with insipid corn niblets and bleached coleslaw. Or maybe it was the restaurant that was wrong. It had the gigantic sanitized atmosphere of Gas Station Standard. The white walls, white Arborite, shiny leatherette, Muzak—the huge emptiness of the place seemed to blend together into one big blank.

"How's your food?" I asked.

"Not bad." He was being charitable. The pierogis were flaccid and bland. As he ate them it even began to snow. All would have been lost if not for the pumpkin pie. I bit into it prepared for the worst, and then the flavour of the filling hit my taste buds. It was tantalizing. Perfect. I began to gobble it greedily. My hands were shaking.

"Are you all right?" asked Hamburg.

"The pie," I said. "It gets fifteen." For a few more seconds Hamburg sat still. Then he leapt from his seat and rushed to the waitress, begging her for a piece of pumpkin pie. The snow thinned and a few minutes later the sun came out. Even the Muzak seemed to fade.

The verdict: terrible for lunch but perfect for an afternoon snack.

Day Two ended with a meal cooked by a friend in Winnipeg. It began with high hopes, with thirty cookbooks on the table and a two-hour wait. At the crucial moment, when the meal came out of the oven, a crisis happened and it turned into grilled cheese sandwiches. Well-intentioned but not inspired. Free. Don't go there uninvited.

Day Three

Breakfast was leftover sandwiches; and lunch, in Keewatin, was easy to forget. It was evening when serious hunger struck again. By this time we were deep in the lake district of northwestern Ontario, on that sweep of highway that curves over Lake Superior.

"Hamburg," I said, "this time you pick the place. The responsibility is too much for me. I'm getting an ulcer."

"There," Hamburg said suddenly. He was pointing to a restaurant on our left, the north side of the highway. Hollet's, it was called. We were 30

miles west of Thunder Bay, near Shabaqua Corners.

There were gas pumps and a shed with a sign saying: Bait For Sale: Minnows But No Worms. This seemed an entirely different kind of place, a supply depot for everything. Once inside we could see that Hollett's was not only a restaurant but also a general store which sold, in addition to food, various sundries, clothes, fishing tackle—even baked goods and paperback books. And, glowing in one corner like a Christmas tree in a dark forest, there was a liquor store outlet.

While Hamburg and I sat at our table and inspected the menu, we eavesdropped.

The man who had served us gas resumed his conversation. He was at the counter, talking to an elderly gentleman about the decline in the tourist business. The elderly gentleman bumped into the waitress as she passed.

"Oh sorry," he said. "I bumped into your waitress."

"That's OK," said the gas man. "I bump into her all the time."

In this restaurant, times had changed for the better. There was almost a complete lack of Arborite and the orange curtains were striped with green. Behind us was a long-haired couple in overalls. They were eating homemade chili and bread. Between mouthfuls the woman turned to her man and said, "If you got white flour, you got starch. If you got brown flour, you got health." The chili was so authentic they were both perspiring.

Meanwhile Hamburg decided to order fish.

"You can't eat fish," I said. "You're a vegetarian."

"Who says," said Hamburg darkly. I ordered soup and roast beef. Hamburg fell in love with the waitress, "She gets fifteen," he kept saying. At the next table three men were discussing a new farm. It was an unusual farm. In fact its owner claimed to be processing rocks for a pet rock seller.

"Always hated having cows," he said. "Too much trouble."

"Damned cows," everyone mumbled.

"I have a machine for washing the rocks," the rock farmer boasted. "They like to get them clean, you know."

"They should have pet spark plugs," a skeptic said. "They'd be easier to carry."

Our soup came. Hamburg, in the throes of love, waxed ecstatic. Mine had real beef in it, and it was thick without being starchy. I gave it ten out of ten.

Meanwhile the farmers went back to talking about rocks.

"You can use them to defend yourself," one of them was saying. "They can't get you for carrying an offensive weapon if it's a pet."

Then the waitress brought my meal. "She's perfect," Hamburg whispered obsessively. "Give her twenty."

"You need a pet rock," I told Hamburg. "Something to have with you, on the road, when things begin to get confused."

I bit into a home-fried potato. It was golden-brown, cooked perfectly throughout. Definitely the best potatoes between Toronto and Edmonton: ten. The beef was thick and tender, the gravy thick and homemade. As I drank the coffee I began to realize that this restaurant was the peak of our journey: the atmosphere, the characters and the food all combined to perfection. I wondered what it would be like to try the whole menu.

Then Hamburg ordered two bizarre-looking pastries.

"Don't do it," I warned nervously. "Don't test our luck."

Hamburg, who had devoured his fish as surreptitiously as possible, now bit into one of the pastries. An unusual look passed across his face. Then he took another bite, much larger. "Thirty," he mumbled. "Who cares about the waitress?"

"Don't talk with your mouth full."

"Tell them to bring doggie bags," Hamburg babbled. "Tell them to buy all the pastry and take it with them."

Day Four

It was lunch the next day before we were hungry again. We were nearing Wawa, Ontario, about halfway between Thunder Bay and the Sault. Wawa is famous for a stuffed goose that lives on a hill overlooking the highway. How it got so fat in Wawa escapes me; it certainly wasn't in

restaurants.

We saw a sign for a restaurant, The Magpie, but the place itself never materialized so we finally gave up and headed into the Heritage Inn Restaurant and Chinese food, a few miles west of Wawa, right beside the OPP Plaza. It was a red brick building with green wood trim, and as we parked outside we saw faces beaming happily through the window.

Inside there was a formal dining room with impressively awful purple chairs and gold table cloths. Luckily it was closed, so we went into the cafeteria section—a cavernous room with four long rows of booths, mostly empty. Even the smiling faces had disappeared.

After a brief intermission, during which I gave Hamburg a pep talk on the value of honest ratings, the waitress appeared, clomping ominously in white nurse shoes, and gave us menus and place mats which had golf courses drawn on them. It's a game: the idea is to put the tip of your pencil at the tee, close your eyes, then try to draw a line ending at the cup. It's harder than it seems but we had lots of time to complete the course before the waitress returned.

"I'll have shrimp with lobster sauce and mushroom fried rice," said Hamburg. These were from the day's specials.

"We don't have those," she said. There was a brief pause. She then walked away. A couple sitting a few booths down from us who must have been tourists too—or else they wouldn't have been there—started to laugh.

"You better be nice to her," the woman said. "You can't ask for things they don't have."

"They were on the menu."

"They don't have any specials today," our good Samaritan said. "Order other things."

The waitress came back. She stood looking over us, tapping her foot.

"I'll have the lake trout," said Hamburg, whose principles had deteriorated.

"We don't have lake trout."

"I thought you only didn't have the specials."

"No," said the waitress. "There's other things we don't have too."

Hamburg ended up with rainbow trout, and I ordered chicken soo guy. When the waitress left us we noticed how the whole place seemed designed to erode hunger. There were four different kinds of light fixtures, nausea-green curtains, and strains of Herb Alpert coming from a radio in the kitchen. The walls were ugly Weldwood paneling and the gift shop was filled with toy Indians dressed in white.

The couple from down the aisle got up to leave and I noticed their meal was mostly uneaten. "Good luck," they said.

A few minutes later the waitress clomped back. "Give her minus ten," Hamburg said as she approached. Her hands wet and covered with bits of flour which dropped off as she set down our plates.

"Here it is," she said. The trout was still twisted with rigor mortis and tasted, Hamburg claimed, like cod liver oil. The chicken soo guy was swimming in so much sauce it didn't taste of anything at all. In fact it began to remind me of my boyhood in Ottawa, of those restaurants that used to be closed down by the health department when they found cats in the refrigerator. I didn't eat very much.

At the till I asked the waitress if I could keep the place mat as a souvenir. "Sure," she said. "Great, aren't they?"

After The Heritage, there was a long and silent afternoon. It was late at night before we decided to risk dinner and stopped at an Esso cafe just east of Thessalon. They served excellent ravioli and raisin pie, but both Hamburg and I were unable to carry on our gastronomic observations. No breakfast on the last day and lunch, at a restaurant at Fesserton—about ninety miles north of Toronto—turned out to be a turkey sandwich made with turkey from a package.

It was nearly three in the afternoon when we finally came to the outskirts of Toronto. There it lay, with 8,000 restaurants vying for our palates. And yet none of them seemed attractive, none exuded that feeling of the total unknown. I realized I had become hooked on small highway restaurants, on their weird, oasis-like atmosphere and the feeling that they were completely stamped and moulded by their owners. And I also realized that somehow I had for the first time survived a trip across the country without feeling as if I had just spent a week on intravenous preservatives.

"Hamburg," I said. "What's the first thing you're going to do when you get to Toronto?"

"Eat," Hamburg said. Some people have no sentiment.

Matt Cohen

Street Cleaning

City men
sweeping the street
outside my apartment

one leans on his broom
eyes roaming
checking

then when he thinks
no one's looking
bends low
edges his hand
under the curb
lifts
holds the sidewalk up
with his one hand
and with the other
gathers up a pile of leaves
and sweeps them
under

Al Pittman

Where to, lady?"

The real surprise—to me anyway—was not really what I did, but how I felt afterwards. Shocked, of course. But not guilty. You might say, and be right, that the very least a woman can be is shocked when she walks out on a sick and blameless husband after forty years. But to feel no guilt at all—feel nothing, in fact, but simple relief and pleasure—that did seem odd, to say the least. How annoying for God (not to mention Adam), after all, if Eve had just walked out of Eden without waiting to be evicted, and left behind her pangs of guilt, as it were, with her leaf apron?

In any case, I just walked out. There was no quarrel with Burt. No crisis at all. The clock chimed nine-thirty. I laid down the breakfast tray carefully (an apple and a cup of cocoa) on the hall desk, and went to my room and packed. Not a word to anyone, even myself, by way of apology or excuse. Why? And why just then? Truly I'm not sure yet, although my name is Eva.

Our house was full of clocks rustling their self-importance and coughing delicately like people in church—they had something to do with it. So did my first old-age pension cheque, which had come the day before like a hint. But what chiefly stopped me was the cold white autumn light pouring through the landing window as I climbed up with the tray. It seemed to bleach the stairway into something like a high white cell. The night before on TV I'd seen cells like that in Viet Nam or somewhere, for political prisoners. You saw them crouched at the bottom of narrow cages, looking up at the light. I've never had a political conviction in my life, unless you count being bored by politics. But there I was just the same. Under bars.

Behind the bedroom door Burt gave his dry, irritable little cough. In a few minutes he would call me in a voice sharp and light with his morning pain. The cup of cocoa on the tray one minute steamed blandly and the next wobbled and slopped itself into the saucer. His mouth would press tight in disgust. "Can't you—" he would say, exasperated, "can't you—"

What I packed first (the whole thing took only ten minutes) was *Wuthering Heights* and a poetry anthology from my bedside shelf; but I didn't forget the grosser animal, and also took along my blood-pressure pills, glasses, hairbrush, and warm old-woman underpants. At the last minute I pulled out the plug of the little FM radio, Neil's birthday present, and tucked it under my arm.

And that was all. Out I went. There was a grey skin puckering on the cocoa as I passed it. On the stairs came his thin voice: "Eva!" I closed the front door on it.

No trouble finding a taxi on Monkland Avenue. Dry, grey October day, touch of frost. Nobody I recognized about. The only hard thing about the whole escape was getting all my possessions—radio, suitcase, and ample rump—crammed into the cab with any kind of dignity. The driver considerately pretended not to notice what a struggle this was. As soon as I got settled and found some breath, I paused to count my money. The pension cheque and fourteen eighty-nine in house money. Not much to kidnap yourself on, to be sure. But enough.

"Where to, lady?" the driver asked.

And of course it was then my legs began to shake. The shaking moved up clear through me, belly and bones. For a minute I thought it might turn into crying or being sick; then with cold hands at my mouth I was astonished to find it was laughter in there, shaking to get out. The driver waited without interest, bored eyes on the traffic.

"Well, you tell me," I said, pressing a Kleenex against my sense of irony. He gave me a wary glance then, and I blew my nose to stop the laughing. Disgraceful. Shocking way to behave, all round. And where to, lady? Where, indeed? I had not given that a single thought. Certainly I couldn't go to Neil and his bitchy elegance of a wife. Or to our few friends who weren't dead or living in Arizona; they would be embarrassed, or scandalized, or both. No; I'd go it alone, and the farther away I could make it, the better. But of course you can't get far on a total of ninety-two eighty-nine, and my own bank account was down to nearly zero after a new winter coat. A bus to somewhere? Or a hotel here for a day or two, until I could get myself organized?

No, because getting organized in a place like the Laurentien Hotel, say, with its Murray's food and rules on every door would simply mean going back.

"No," I said out loud and put away the Kleenex. The driver waited resignedly. "Just drive downtown, will you?" The engine gnashed its teeth and we shot forward. "Right downtown—somewhere near St. Lawrence Main." Because now that I was collecting my wits a bit, I realized someone from Notre Dame de Grâce couldn't find a better place to hide than the other side of Montreal. I could find a room somewhere in the crowded French east end, and it would do perfectly. As for later on, and what to do then, I hadn't the least idea. I sat back on the cab's torn upholstery and we skimmed away through the neat, respectable rows of prosperous flats, full of decent women at their custodial jobs—wheeling babies, raking leaves, lugging bags of food. And I waited to feel guilty, properly horrified at what I was doing. Nothing at all stirred except a quite objective interest in what would happen next. Not to have the faintest idea what I might do—or become—was a peculiarly new and interesting experience, all by itself.

from *The Book of Eve*, by Constance Beresford-Howe

I'm not interested in age. People who tell their ages are silly. You're as young as you feel.

Elizabeth Arden
Ontario-born cosmetic queen

About the only good thing you can say about old age is, it's better than being dead!

Stephen Leacock

Neighbours

The street where I live is divided by fences so it seems more crowded than it really is.
Actually, the lots are huge—twenty-five, twenty-seven feet.
Most of the shanties have a large screened veranda and a master bedroom big enough for a brass bed that sleeps six people easily, with leftover space for a kitchen chair to put your clothes on.
Of course, the bedroom window is a bit small.
A good thing. Because it saves on the heat.
But however it is, the window is too much for Mrs. Kolosky's nerves.
The trouble is, every time she turns to sleep on her right side, Mrs. Weinstein's fence stabs her in the eyes.
Why couldn't it be karagana or lilac or wooden laths?
Why did it have to be something classy like a galvanized iron fence?
Mrs. Kolosky's fence didn't pretend to be classy—just ordinary chicken wire and sweetpeas laced with white string, the kind that comes from a bobbin hanging over the cash register of any grocery store.
Take the fence, says Mrs. Kolosky.
I am sleeping blind on my right side.
So? answers Mrs. Weinstein.
Sleep on the left side.
The fence stands.
The feud between Mrs. Weinstein and Mrs. Kolosky started with the stubborn old maple growing sideways.
Or maybe it was something else.
Who knows?
Maybe Mrs. Kolosky was jealous of the Weinstein fence, a double row of iron spears which *They* said Mr. Weinstein salvaged from a catholic-bleeding-heart cemetery where monuments and fences are moving out to make room for the lawnmowers.
All the same it was very suspicious.
Like a dying man's curse, the root of Mrs. Kolosky's maple, growing sideways, came up between the Weinstein radishes and nothing could change it.
Your maple is showing me five fingers, says Mrs. Weinstein over the fence.
And that's exactly how it looked, one fat root the size of your thumb and four smaller roots with the thumb pointing at Mrs. Weinstein.
Did I tell the maple go into the Weinstein

radishes and show five fingers? asks Mrs.
Kolosky. The tree has his own brains.
Where he wants to go, he goes.
It's a free country.
Never mind the free country, says Mrs.
Weinstein. I am giving you one month, just one
month for the apology.
If not, goodbye charlie.
Friends we never was, the friendship is ended.
Ha Ha Ha, says Mrs. Kolosky.
So much for the apology.
After that, stranger and stranger things began to
happen.
Mrs. Kolosky's hexed chickens started laying eggs
with bloodshot eyeballs.
Mr. Weinstein's socks, hanging on the clothesline,
had all the toes cut off.
Mrs. Kolosky threw a washbasin of potato peels
over the fence.
Mrs. Weinstein threw back, accidentally on
purpose, a basin of chicken guts.
And the very next morning, Mrs. Weinstein,
expecting a maple-leaf lard can with fresh-picked
blueberries, put her hand in the pail, four inches
of cow manure, the compliments of you know who.
Even if they could avoid each other, they didn't.
In fact, it was the other way around
With her arms crossed over her apron, Mrs.

Weinstein stood at the fence for hours, waiting for
Mrs. Kolosky to come out into the yard.
Or Mrs. Kolosky, waiting for Mrs. Weinstein to
come out, stood at the clothesline for hours,
beating the carpet to death with the broom, until
she got her chance.
Dirty foreigner, says Mrs. Kolosky, looking up at
the sky.
The same to you and many of them, says Mrs.
Weinstein looking up at the sky.
The days came, the days went and the feud kept
going on.
It might still be going on if it wasn't for the new
neighbour.
Just before Green Holiday, a moving truck drove
up in front of Semenko's blue and yellow house
sold for taxes.
Every third house on the street is blue and yellow,
the colors of the Ukrainian flag.
Out of the truck came a woman, and a boy,
looking about nine years old, in a skimpy jacket
and strange gold buttons with anchors and
crowns.
Boze, Boze, says Mrs. Kolosky (translation: God
God):
More foreigners already.
English yet.
The worst kind.

Poor woman, says Mrs. Weinstein.
You should know from her pasty white face, she is eating only English white bread and suet.
Suet, I use for lighting candles to Our Virgin Mary, answers Mrs. Kolosky.
But for eating, like you say it, Mrs. Weinstein.
Oy Vay (no translation available):
What the poor orphans are crying for is a pot of healthy red borsch.
Faah on borsch, says Mrs. Weinstein.
For curing anything and Everything, the chicken soup is first.
Not to mention the overcoat, says Mrs. Kolosky.
The boy could be using a warm overcoat.
And why not the overcoat from my brother Dmitri, brand new second hand, size 46, with plenty to grow on?
And for the little mother, felt boots, Oiving Monahan's drygoods, $1.98.
What you think?
$1.98 is good, says Mrs. Weinstein.
98 cents is better.
Tomorrow we go to see drygoods and jew down the Monahan.
That was the end of the feud, no harm done.
And there they are as close as lice: Mrs. Weinstein, Mrs. Kolosky and Mrs. Brittannia, sitting on Mrs. Kolosky's verandah, spitting sunflower seeds in the friendly autumn of old comrades.

from *The Street Where I Live*, by Maara Haas

I like a little bit of everything. A little bit of lovin', a little bit of drinkin', and a little bit of workin'. I watch out pretty careful every day for banana peels.

Ma Murray
pioneer BC newspaperwoman

Toronto Italian: New World Language

Toronto's 400,000 Italian-Canadians are proudly independent. They hate to borrow money—but they have no such hangups about borrowing words.

Any Canadian who has become the boiffrendi or ghellaffrendi of a young Italian and has sat on the cesterfilde in the dainirummo or the frontirummo of their home wondering how they will manage linguistically with the rest of the family is likely to discover they can have an interesting conversation with the sisteralo or broderalo about their life in aiscuola.

For twenty-five years, Italian immigrants have been demonstrating their common-sense attitude to language problems by borrowing the words they needed.

Most often it began at work where early immigrants, who came mainly from the rural south of Italy, had little or no formal education and no contact with city life and industrial jobs.

They simply didn't have the words so they listened and borrowed and added a few Italian-sounding endings and the result is a way of speech that enables Italian workers to deal with the bosso on the giobba whether they are a lebura or a formenni or whether they drive a buldoza or a crena or lay bricchi on pisiguorco (piece-work).

Now their children are at university—and are starting the process of unlearning this new mixed language, or at least learning how to say the same things in standard Italian.

There are between 1,500 and 2,000 Italian-Canadian students at the University of Toronto, most of them enrolled in the department of Italian studies.

For many, one of their early courses is one that teaches them the difference between Italo-Canadian Italian and pure Italian and gives them practice in using the language without all its English borrowings.

The course was made possible by a study done by Domenico Pietropaolo and his wife Laura Springolo, who both teach in the department. Mr. Pietropaolo made a collection of over 1,000 "loan words" while he was working at the Centro Organizzativo Italiano, a grass roots community organization helping working-class Italians. Now he and his wife teach the course and wean Italo-Canadian students away from the language they grew up with.

At the end of it, they won't talk about taking a bucco off the bucciselfi to read in the bacchi-iarda or the fronti-iarda or the basamento.

Nor will they talk about starting the day with a brecchifesti of becon or amma with slice of ciso and when they go to the drive-in, they won't discuss whether to put grevi or checciappa (ketchup) on their frencifrai—always assuming, of course, that they don't order a bag of pappacorna or pinozze (peanuts).

When they go shopping, they won't call at the drogghistoro or the sciustoro (shoe-store) to buy buzzi (boots) or the becheri to buy a lofo and when they drive they won't talk about fare un raitti (make a right hand turn) or a fare a leffiti at the end of the stritto or the aiguei (highway).

It may be hard to stop eating aisi crimmi or wearing bluginsi or putting erpinsi in their hair or mecappa on their faces.

It may be hard at times to remember not to say sori (sorry) or ariappa (hurry up) or caman (come on) or that the telephone line is bisi and to stop calling the building in Nathan Phillips Square "sitiolla."

But it will put the students in the mainstream of Italian speech and Mr. Pietropaolo says they don't mind relearning the new vocabulary, even though old habits sometimes die hard.

But there is one word that may outlast the others. There is no standard Italian for that shoppers' wonderland at Bathurst and Bloor, and so future generations of Italian-Canadian doctors and lawyers may still talk about taking a trip to Onesteddi on Saturday afternoon.

Norman Hartley

The Candyman's Cart

The candyman's cart has broken down,
He's standing on the sidewalk holding a wheel,
His cashews and pistachios, they cover the ground,
He's scratchin' his head, you know how he feels.
Off to see some sweet tooth
On the far side of town,
The candyman's cart has broken down.

The candyman's cart has broken down
Distracted by a fatal whim,
In the instant he turned around
This traffic became a dangerous thing.
Off to see some sweet tooth
On the far side of town
The candyman's cart has broken down

The candyman's cart has broken down
On the sunniest day of the year,
What he thought was good fortune flying around
Was only those pigeons drawing near.
Off to see some sweet tooth
On the far side of town
The candyman's cart has broken down.

The candyman's cart has broken down,
He fills the metre with the day's receipts,
His windmills and chestnuts cover the ground,
He shrugs his shoulders and paces the street.
Off to see some sweet tooth
On the far side of town
The candyman's cart has broken down.

Joe Hall, from his record, *impuls(e)*, Vol. 5, No. 2

. April 6/77

constitutes
...ics for
...out along
...for
...ers,

Joe Hall

P.S. — please check the amendments
in copies.

Visible and Invisible in Canada

For a Commonwealth citizen like me, becoming Canadian took no more than five minutes in an unpretentious office. A maternal French Canadian official insisted over my protests that Indian citizens were British subjects. In the end I undid the work of generations of martyred freedom fighters, pledged loyalty to the British Queen, and became a Canadian citizen.

But in Canada I feel isolated, separate in the vastness of this underpopulated country. I cannot bring myself to snowshoe or ski. Unspoiled nature terrifies me, I have not yet learned the words to the national anthem. I tell myself I shall never make friends here, though, in truth, I am lying; I am unlikely to make friends in any country.

In Canada I am both too visible and too invisible. I am brown; I cannot disappear in a rush-hour Montreal crowd. The media had made me self-conscious about racism. I detect arrogance in the slow-footedness of sales clerks. At lunch, in the faculty club, I am not charmed when colleagues compliment me for not having a "singsong" accent. I am tired of being exotic, being complimented for qualities of voice, education, bearing, appearance, that are not extraordinary.

But if as a citizen I am painfully visible, I cannot make myself visible at all as a Canadian writer. The literary world in Canada is nascent, aggressively nationalistic, and self-engrossed. Reviewers claim that my material deals with Indians usually in India, and because my publisher is American, my work is of no interest to Canadian writers and readers.

In Canada I am the wife of a well-known Canadian writer who "also writes," though people often assume it is in Bengali. In order to be recognized as an Indian-born Canadian writer, I would have to convert myself into a token figure, write abusively about local racism and make Brown Power fashionable.

But I find I cannot yet write about Montreal. It does not engage my passions. It is caught up in passion all its own, it renders the Asian immigrant whose mother tongue is neither French nor English more or less irrelevant. Montreal merely fatigues and disappoints.

And so I am a late-blooming colonial who writes in a borrowed language (English), lives permanently in an alien country (Canada), and publishes in and is read, when read at all, in another alien country, the United States.

My Indianness is fragile; it has to be professed and fought for, even though I look so unmistakably Indian. Language transforms our ways of apprehending the world; I fear that my decades-long use of English as a first language has cut me off from my desh (country) . . .

Prior to this year-long stay in India, I had seen myself as others saw me in Montreal, a brown woman in a white society, different, perhaps even special, but definitely not a part of the majority.

I receive, occasionally, crazy letters from women students at McGill accusing me of being "mysterious," "cold," "hard to get to know," and the letter writers find this mysteriousness offensive. I am bothered by these letters, especially by the aggressive desire of students to "know" me. I explain it as a form of racism.

The unfamiliar is frightening; therefore I have been converted into a "mystery." I can be invested with powers and intentions I do not possess.

Bharati Mukherjee, from *Days and Nights in Calcutta*, by Clark Blaise and Bharati Mukherjee

The Poor We Have With Us Always

It is funny how the infant mind functions.

I can mind, when I was small, being lodged off down on the coats in the back of the school at dances.

This is where they put you at about two o'clock in the night when you commenced to get groggy and wanted a nap. There was a row of desks shoved in tight to the wall for all hands to put their coats on.

Sometimes there would be three or four of us at once laid out down there heads and tails, some on a half-doze, more with their thumbs stuck in their gob looking around, and others a cold junk sleeping it off.

Solid comfort.

I can recall hearing this very restful "RUMP-A-RUMP-A-RUMP" noise in the background. It was half a shuffle and half a stamp which caused the floor to heave rhythmically up and down and rattled a few loose panes in the windows.

And I remember watching the light from the kerosene oil lamps dancing on the ceiling from the draft as they all swung around in the Reel and I can remember this strange noise threading through everything, rising and falling in tune with the flickering light.

The big puzzle occupying my infant noggin was: Is that noise making the light or is that light making the noise?

That is the first thing I can ever remember about dances.

She Came Down into A Flat

Of course, before many more years had passed I had put two and two together and figured out that this noise was coming from the fiddler regardless of what he played upon. Even a rack comb and tissue paper.

First they had the Sale of Work. Second, they had the First Table followed by the Second and Third Tables depending on how many was there. Then they might have a Guess Cake or Grab Bags and third they had the Dance.

Sale of Work was cloths and aprons and pillow slips hung across on lines and all worked out into cock sparrows and roses and double mitts, fancy for Sundays, and cushion tops all made mostly out of dyed wool and flour bags bleached out.

You never saw many figgy buns flung about at the First Table. There was always a steadier lot sitting in at it. They even had grace at First which had to do for the Second and Third Tables too where you had more driving works and carrying on.

A Mug-Up In Paradise

They used to sing grace.

Every word was stretched out to the extent of an elastic garter. This was because the Salvationers had the name of singing too fast while the Church of Englanders were known to drain through their noses.

When both got together the Salvationers started out dead slow in defence to the C of Es and the C of Es slowed her down even a notch more to prove that the Salvationers *were* racy.

It was the most dismal thing you ever heard. "Beeeeeprezzzzzent aayt oour taay-ble Lord" and so on through, "Be here and everywhere adored; Thy creatures bless and grant that we; May feast in Paradise with Thee."

"AAAAAWWWWWMMMMMENNNNNNNN."

Then the Catholics from Southern Harbour blessed theirselves and all hands sat down and dug in.

Behaving The Same As You Ought

Generally, they had Meat Teas or Soup Suppers.

This was bully beef and potato salad of different sorts. Then jelly and blanc mange and partridge berry tarts and cakes and figgy buns and tea.

If someone who had a few drinks in, or some of the youngsters hove a bun at someone at the other end of the table or flicked blanc mange on their spoons across, then one of the women serving on the table would give them a click across the ear and tell them to behave the same as they ought.

When they had Soup Suppers you got a chance to be sent down to the house for the boiler.

Halfways up with it yourself and the other chap put down the boiler, took off the cover and drove your arm down to rummage a biggish bit of meat off the bottom.

This was a tricky business.

You had to be quick because they were timing you back at the school. If you took too much they would notice it because meat wasn't always that plentiful. And the stuff was burning hot.

So it was in and out of the boiler as quick as you could and then jam your arm down in the snow to take the sting out. Once, Gordon lost his mitt in the boiler and forgot to hook it out and got a lacing for it.

Doggedy, Doggedy, Bark At The Cat

When the Last Table was nearly eat down to a shambles they started the dance.

Mostly they had sets which included such things as "Form a Line and Advance," "Dance to Your Partner" and "Round the House." Sometimes they had "the Reel" or the "furginia Reel" and in later years, a "Wallace."

Everyone got out except for the small youngsters and women not feeling well. The oldish men were always the ring leaders of it. It seemed that the fiddler played a lot faster than Harry Hibbs.

There were two sides to a set and when one side stopped the other side commenced. To my knowledge, there is no harder or faster or longer dancing in the world unless among uncivilized races.

The windows were up with the snow blowing in, the door was open, the stove was let die down but whenever the fiddler stopped the men in their shirtsleeves with sweat running down their backs would lurch for the door and fall across the bridge rail outside with the steam flying out of them in the frost.

And the women panting for breath with their hands to their bosoms would stagger off toward the kitchen to dip a cup in the water barrel. They would shake their heads at the other women in

the kitchen and puff their cheeks and say, "Ohmygod! I'm just about dead."

The Reel was even worse. When someone would mention having the Reel there would be groans all around and people saying, "Oh, no, not the Reel. For God's sake not the Reel." Reels took an hour or more apiece.

Mussels in The Corner

As a lad I was somewhat on the slight side. It is only these late years that I have fallen into flesh. So one of my worries then was that a woman might take me off my feet in the dances.

Some of them were upwards of seventeen stone. There were very few there that any husky man could swing off their feet so generally it worked out to a tie. But imagine getting taken off your feet yourself!

Once I had like to but that was on account of the water they had sprinkled on the floor to keep down the dust making into ice down by where the door was open.

When you got swinging about 102 miles an hour they commenced to tighten their grip until you could feel your ribs lap over and your draft cut off and little spots dancing in front of your eyes.

If two people swinging happened to rouse into two more some bad injuries were likely to result. If you let go at top speed you would clear the floor like an oblong bowling ball and probably have to be dug out of the wall.

Only the poorest kind of dances ever finished up before it was daylight all abroad.

The Poor We Have With Us Always

By means of these affairs they built schools, churches and halls, assisted distressed persons, sent parcels overseas and helped put a stitch of clothes on the poor naked backs of heathens in other countries who, although odd looking, are created in our blessed Saviour's image just the very same as you and me.

Once when I was telling a person from upalong about Soup Suppers and so forth he shook his head and became down in the mouth and said: "You must have been very poor."

Strange talk. If we had been poor it would have been the other way around. People in other countries would have been running off Soup Suppers to send parcels over to us.

It is funny how the mainland mind functions.

from *You May Know Them as Sea Urchins, Ma'am*, by Ray Guy

By Sid Adilman

Author rides Depression wav[e]

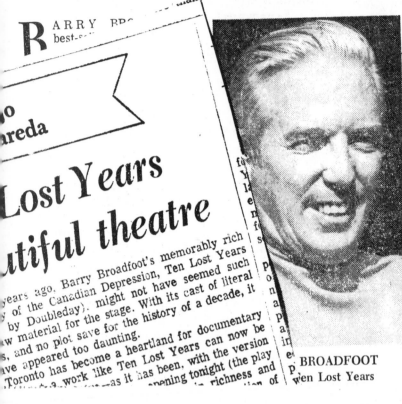

BROADFOOT
[T]en Lost Years

ARRY BR[OADFOOT]
best-s[eller]

[Toront]o
[B]areda

Lost Years
[bea]utiful theatre

[ye]ar[s] ago, Barry Broadfoot's memorably rich [histor]y of the Canadian Depression, Ten Lost Years [published] by Doubleday), might not have seemed such [ra]w material for the stage. With its cast of literal [humanity], and no plot save for the history of a decade, it [might h]ave appeared too daunting.

[But] Toronto has become a heartland for documentary [dr]ama, [and] a work like Ten Lost Years can now be [produced]—as it has been, with the version [op]ening tonight (the play ... richness and ...

duced," s[a] CBC-TV is bringing [it] mid-Februa[ry] pearance.
"The boo[k] success," [...] amazed a[t] should hav[e] as I was [al]ways a w[ar] wave; the[y] now—the [...] picked up [...] cr[...]
rid[...] sec[...] the [...]
"[...] hist[ory] beca[me] com[ing] ning[...] neer[...]
Te[n Lost] lishe[d] CBC-[...]

CBC dram[a] termed 'garb[age'?]

OTTAWA (CP) — The CBC was accused F[or] the public obscenity, profanity and "gift-wra[pping]" in its television drama programs.

Members of the Commons broadcast comm[ittee] to CBC President Laurent Picard that the [...] television and radio system spen[d] [...] tizing the tribulations [...] unhappily [...]

Emotional tale of hard times

By Nancy Russell
of the Star-Phoenix

The 1930s may have been Ten Lost Years but people, [...] lived and experienced [...] ed strengths

the prairie winds and drought. Men, [...] children working [...] wages and frei[ght] crawling with hobo[s] a people despera[te, bro]ken. The laughte[r over] the sore muscle[s ...] [j]ourneys are [...]

[T]en Lost Years—a vivid evocation for Canad[a]

By CHRISTOPHER DAFOE
Sun Drama Critic

[The] Great Depression of 1929-1939 [...] [stoo]d, until quite recently [...] [i]n the Canadi[an ...] that it [...]

[r]aw life in the dirty thirties

[BEN]NY SMITH
[a]f reporter

[Ten L]ost Years, [...musi]cal, [...]

with the local social worker, in order to obtain dole.
the R.B. Bennett, [prime] minister was blamed

The cast were superb in singing Cedric Smith's songs.
At times the musical was [hea]vy. Never the less, [Lo]st Years is still good [enterta]inment.
[...]members Dita Faabo, [...]e Chick Roberts, [...s]... Skene,

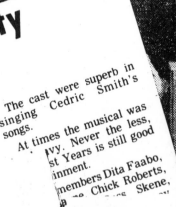

The Leader-Post, Regina, Saturday, Octo[ber ...]

[T]en Lost Years still a haunting theatrical evening

If, in the modest but heartening recent history of [C]anadian drama, the Toron-[t]o [...] Productions' [...] [Ten] [Lost] Years [...]

the Broadfoot text—Smith has expanded our notions of the lyric theatre in subtle and memorable ways.
And an enormous cheer, [...] for director George [...] who on two oc-[casions] [...] actors

Ten Lost Years almost too ener[getic]

By LYNN SHERVILL
of The Leader-Post

If you've read the standard [C]anadian history texts, it's [ha]rd to understand how any-[one] can take 10 years from [...] pages — 10 lost years at [...]

should somehow detract from the production.
It was often hard to resolve the conflict which emerged from an obviously young and spirited cast recalling an era now associated with those 45 years of age and older

use of [...] noise [...] aged [...] three [...] can ju[mp] train w[...] stage.

Buying A Human Being

We moved to Montreal in 1933 and we found what we were looking for the first day, a perfectly lovely house in Westmount. There were houses for rent or for lease and you could buy them, everywhere. While we waited for our furniture to come out from the coast we all stayed at the Ritz. A grand hotel then, and it still is.

I phoned an employment agency and told them I wanted some staff and they asked a few questions and the next day a woman came over to the hotel. I told her I knew nothing about running a house and I wanted the best servants she could find. We drove over to the house and she worked it out this way. A chef and a woman who could be my maid and also serve the meals, and two domestics and a yardman, we had perfectly huge grounds, and a laundress who would come in Monday, Wednesday and Friday.

When our furniture moved in, this agency had people for us. The chef got $40 a month and his board and room. My maid got $30 and board and room. The first domestic maid got $25 and the second maid got $15. The gardener, and he was the chauffeur too if we wanted it, he got $25. The laundress got two dollars a day, and she scrubbed by hand and ironed by hand and she lived at home. I paid her carfare too. Ten cents a day. Perfectly ridiculous, isn't it? Buying a human being, an excellent chef, for $10 a week, or a small maid for 50 cents a day. Nobody thought anything of it.

as told to Barry Broadfoot in *Ten Lost Years*

The Comics House

We lived in Hamilton and my Dad got laid off from the steel company, and he went down to Nova Scotia to look for work in a mill there. So when he was gone my mother and me and my sister Annie moved up to stay with her younger brother who lived in a shack near a dump. I remember it was at the end of a street car line east of Toronto somewhere.

Well, we never heard a word from Dad anymore, he just disappeared. Dis-ap-peared. Gone. Then my uncle was arrested and sent to jail for breaking into a boxcar, and that left Mom and me and Annie in this little shack. This was around 1936 and it was fall and getting colder so we sent into the dump and we got dozens of these

Heinz beans and spaghetti and other cardboard boxes and Annie and I held and Mom nailed them all around the inside of the shack. It just had one big room and she figured that would help keep out the cold.

We got some food from the dump, the stuff restaurants and hospitals put out. It was mostly bread and cake and potatoes that if you cut enough you could cut out the rot, and there were jam pails and if you boiled water in them they'd come clean and you had a good sweetener. People around were doing this.

I found a big bundle of comics tied together and brought it home and mother said it would make good insulation too, so she got a pot of glue made of flour and water and we papered the walls with these comics, the Katzenjammer Kids and Little Orphan Annie and Tarzan of the Apes and Buck Rogers. The word got around that the Turnbulls had a house made of comics. They called it the Comics House. Kids used to come from all over the area and they'd just walk around, on the cots, kneeling on the table, standing up, and they'd read these pasted up comic strips. I noticed that the kids would make rude remarks about Little Orphan Annie so we pasted her over.

Really, that shack was getting like a social club. Grown-ups, the parents of the kids, used to come over at night and there would be talk, about politics, Mackenzie King, Mussolini, the depression, although I don't think that's what it was called. Our shack was a social club. Men would bring wood for the stove and sometimes a woman would bring some cookies or something.

One little guy, he must have been eighty, he came to the door one afternoon and he had a note and my mother read it and it said, would someone read the comics to him. He couldn't read but he sure could look. Every week, once a week he'd come and one of us, or one of the kids who were there, would read him a wall of comics and he'd laugh and go away happy. He must have read the same comics fifteen times that winter but it never made any difference. He was an old, old man and he just wanted company.

One afternoon when he left he gave my mother two one dollar bills, all grimy and creased. Oh, by the way, he never spoke. She didn't want to take the money but he just kept pushing her hand back. Mother figured that was the only money he had to his name but we'd helped him pass a tough winter and he was just showing his gratitude.

as told to Barry Broadfoot in *Ten Lost Years*

Hard Times Killed My Man

The coal killed my man. Just as sure as if he'd been on the field of battle, through shot and shell. He worked for a coal company, first in Winnipeg and then we came to Toronto where my relatives were. This was 1935. Hard times, I assure you. Nobody wants them again. Why my husband couldn't do anything else but haul coal I will never know.

You had this truck. In Winnipeg it was painted yellow and it had a box and you loaded it with these sacks with bulky coal, it would stick out everywhere and push into his back, and then you drove to the house which wanted the coal and you carried each sack to the chute. My man used to say each sack weighed 125 pounds, sixteen to the ton, and you parked in the lane and it was a sixty foot walk to the chute and you had to make your own path and the snow always was two feet deep. When you're hauling coal, what else have you to think about. He could count to sixteen, all right.

Home after dark, maybe seven or eight loads on an ordinary day, and he got $2.50 a day. His pay packet on Saturday night was $15. About sixty a month for the hardest work one man ever ordered another man to do. He'd come home and I'd say, "You look like a coal man," because his face would be black with dust and he'd say, if he had the strength, "No, I look like a whipped nigger."

He would be strong at the start of winter because in summer they just hauled ice and that was simple, easy, and the pay was the same. Ice door to door was a vacation. But you could just see him running down in winter. How many's the time, oh hundreds, that he has just lain down on the kitchen floor and I'd be taking off his wool jacket and pants and one of the kids would be working away on his boots. The dinner would be steaming on the table and the dear man would say, "Eat, it'll get cold." Sometimes he'd have a bowl of vegetable soup and some bread and then go to bed and sleep right through, not a movement, not a whisper until next morning. Ten, eleven hours of the sleep of the dead.

How could there be a man-wife relationship that way? The man never saw his children. He slept all day Sunday, or just stared out the window. He never cursed. By God, I did though. I used to go to church and I'd curse Mr. Bennett, the prime minister, and then when he was out, I'd curse King, the new one.

In 1939 my man fell and with this load of coal on his back something snapped. The doctor said he couldn't do hard work again, so the company hemmed and hawed and finally put him in as a checker. He weighed the trucks and filled out cards, but it was no use. He just kept going down and down and although he was only 33, the army wouldn't have him. He wanted to go, for his country. His own country didn't want him. Bad back. They had a name that long (*she holds her arms out wide*) for what he had, and that was it. He died next year. That's how the hard times destroyed my man. And me.

as told to Barry Broadfoot in *Ten Lost Years*

Hunkies In Town

My father was a doctor. We were Polish. He was and mother too, but the kids were born in Canada. What's that make us?

We'd lived in this town in Saskatchewan but it wasn't big enough to support two doctors. It was dying, you see. Dad was the youngest of the two doctors so he pulled up stakes and we moved to a nice town in Ontario. My brothers and family still live there, not too far from London.

It was wall to wall Anglo-Saxon. Scotch, English, United Empire Loyalist. Presbyterian and Anglican. We didn't even have a church to go to.

The people were very kind. A new doctor, a young doctor in town and they needed one badly so we got the real treatment. People can be very kind, you know, and Dad was soon in practice and Mom had some new friends and we were in school and when Dad asked for a loan to buy a house, the down payment, the bank came through just like that. Easy.

Dad had a brother in Alberta who wasn't doing

well and so he wrote him and told him there was plenty of work for him. He could be his partner. Uncle Andrew came and his family and then his wife's cousin was leaving Dundurn, burned out, and he was going to the coast but my dad and uncle persuaded him to come east and he set up on a farm right on the edge of town. See the pattern? Here was a good place, and now there were three Polish families, and a year and a half before there were none.

The cousin bought a little feed and grain store on Main Street and one day Dad and Uncle Andrew and this cousin Nick are standing outside in the sun talking and I'm walking by the bank and this banker who lent Dad the money, he is with a friend and he points down where my dad is talking with his brother and he says, "Looks like the miserable hunkies are taking over this whole town."

That's the way it was. I remember that about the depression. I was upset and I told Dad and he was upset and he said to me: "I guess that proves we'll just have to be twice as good citizens as anybody else."

as told to Barry Broadfoot in *Ten Lost Years*

Long Before Pearl Harbour

I was born in Vancouver in 1902 so I have the advantage of looking at the problem from three sides—from my parents' side because they were born in Japan, and from my side as a Canadian, and third, also from dealing with Japanese and Canadian people all those years.

People really know nothing of our problem. They only think of the evacuation of the people, the 27,000 people, in 1942. A terrible thing, people say. Too bad. Yes. Yes, but a good thing too. It broke up the ghetto concentration of the Japanese people around Vancouver, they moved to the interior, to the prairies, to Toronto and they began new lives. They began new careers. They became successful.

The non-Japanese think that the attack on Pearl Harbour, the declaration of war, the British and American and Canadian involvement in the Pacific war was the reason for the evacuation of March, 1942, and the internment camps. No, that was not the whole reason. That was the excuse. The decision to move the people out had been made before that. The decision had actually been made in 1940 and the studies to arrive at this conclusion had begun years earlier. In the 1930s, the Japanese government's war on China had been the excuse then and the politicians were just waiting for the right time. The Pearl Harbour attack was the perfect excuse.

If you look underneath it all, back of it all, it was economic. You see, we were Japanese. Canadians, but still Japanese. Look at our size. Small, aren't we? Our skin. Dark. Not white. We weren't white men. Only about half spoke English, and while there were thousands of

The photographs are of the play based on Barry Broadfoot's oral history of the Great Depression, Ten Lost Years. The 1974 drama produced by Toronto Workshop Productions was written by Perth County "Conspirator" Cedric Smith and playwright Jack Winter.

The play was performed in cities and towns across Canada, as well as in Europe. Responses ranged from great enthusiasm to indignant condemnation. To some in the audience it evoked memories of their own experiences of hard times. To others it exaggerated the difficulties lived through by Canadian during those ten lost years.

Members of the cast who appear in the photographs are: Peter Millard, Grant Roll, Ross Skene, Diane Douglas, Francois-Regis Klanfer, Rich Payne, Judy Crocker, Jim Warburton, Heather Ritchie, Rosemary Dunsmore, Sandy Crawley, Dita Paabo, Suzette Couture, Peter Faulkner, Michael Burgess, and Chick Roberts.

German and Italian and Chinese and even French in British Columbia who couldn't read a newspaper in English, we were in the wrong because we were Japanese.

It goes back into the 1880s when we first came. We didn't segregate ourselves. The whites, what you would call the red necks, the politicians, they segregated us. We set up our own schools because how else could our children learn? Our own churches, Christian, but also our own religion, yes. Newspaper. Meeting halls. Restaurants, hotels. Stores. Where else could we get our food, the things our old people wanted, the food that

was favourable to our diet? Yes, we became a ghetto.

A Japanese is a good fisherman. There is something about fishing which makes him good or better than anyone. The whites, through laws and pressure, tried to force us out of the fishing through the twenties and thirties. Our women could work in the cannery because they were so fast and efficient, not because they were wanted as Canadians. Even the Chinese were against us. Naturally so, I guess. Old hatreds stretch back through the centuries.

We moved into the woods to work, and laws and brutality forced us out. Farms. The Japanese are excellent farmers. Vegetables. Each little plant is treated with care, with tenderness, fertilized and watered. If we had the land, we could not be forced out. A farm which might support two families would have six, and everybody worked from dawn to dark and there, that was the way vegetable prices were kept so low. The same with stores. Wholesaling, tailoring, laundries. Undercut the white competition. You had to to survive. Live in the back of the stores, three or four families in two or three rooms.

It was the whites who forced the Japanese into this position where the white businessman could no longer compete. The Japanese was forced into the worst kind of labour.

Do you know that the 1930s, the period you are asking about, most of the Japanese in British Columbia were Canadian citizens. Born in Canada. Canadian citizens. But we couldn't do this and we couldn't do that. First, we couldn't vote. Yes, we couldn't vote. A Japanese man with a doctor's degree couldn't serve in the provincial legislature, and neither could the market gardener. No Japanese could. Or be an alderman, or a school trustee. You couldn't be a hand logger or a lawyer. Not a druggist. You couldn't work for the government either, even with a shovel on the roads. You couldn't serve on a jury. You don't think this is possible? It is.

I don't say there was all that hatred by all the people but this was the depression, and things hadn't really been too good in the province for years anyway, and people saw the Japanese-Canadians as a threat. An economic threat. Somebody who just might, just might take a dollar a week out of your pocket by being a sharper businessman, a harder farm worker, a faster stuffer in a cannery. And I don't need to tell you, it doesn't have to go much further than that to translate this economic fear into action. What kind of action? Political action. Kick them out.

A report called the Special Committee on Orientals in British Columbia was published in autumn of 1940, *a year before* Pearl Harbour. This report said there was a great hatred of the Japanese by the whites in British Columbia. The report could not back up its findings with any specific instances, just that there was a great hatred. They said the Japanese were underselling, undercutting their white Canadian competitors. What is competition all about? What we have in the supermarkets now? Do you call that competition? That is monopoly. The report also talked about great smuggling of Japanese nationals in to Canada through B.C., and they talked about spies mapping the coast. This was proved over and over again to be rubbish, so what they came up with was that the Japanese had to be protected from the whites. So they must all be kept in a position of surveillance, watched by the authorities, registered. No military training, because they were not to be trusted. You see what this did, don't you? When the war with the Japanese did come along, the Japanese were all lined up, so to speak, located, numbered, marked, ready to go.

One thing to be said for the committee, its members were not unanimous, but the anti-Japanese obviously were in the majority.

You will have a hard time convincing any Japanese of my generation that all this was not economic, that those whose ox was being gored were not screaming the loudest. A shameful, disgraceful period, and the true story still has to be told. But, shameful as it was, the Japanese accepted it with courage and honour and for that, more credit to them all. For many, as I've said before, it did open up a whole new world, but that was a fortunate end result.

It was never my intention to mean that all the white people were bad, or against us. That definitely was not the case. But that type were there in sufficient number and they made enough noise and the time was ready for them, and there were enough politicians who saw in it a means of getting votes. And this, mind you, at a time when from the docks of New Westminster and Vancouver ship loads of scrap iron were being sent to Japan, and the politicans knew that metal would be used in munitions and that Japan had lined up with Italy and Germany as an ally. That's a politician for you. There are still a few of these men around. I wonder if they have changed. If the faction of west coast Canadians who were against us in those days had had their way, our children and grandchildren would still be working in coal mines. As slaves.

as told to Barry Broadfoot, in *Ten Lost Years*

My hands tremble
As I sign my naturalization papers
Making me a Canadian citizen
and Canada my final resting place

Takeo Nakano,
Japanese-born Canadian

Honkey Red

I don't have a back porch,
And I don't have a rocking chair,
Got a dirty old coat and a shaky hand,
And a face like a grizzly bear,
I'm an old wino, and I scare all the ladies,
As you might say I'm a bum,
But I'm sure wired up to the Honkey Red,
And that good Gold Anchor rum.
When I need a drink, I'm stains on a sink,
I'm please and thank you, ma'am,
But when I've got a head full of Honkey Red
Then I don't give a good God damn.

Well I fought in your wars, now I sleep in your doors,
And I left my leg in France,
And all that remains is a ghostly pain,
When the mornings get too damp,
I was born in the sticks, and I got Grade 6,
So I ain't much in demand,
I deliver handbills and I steal red pills
For the boys in the whorehouse band.

When I need a drink I'm stains on a sink
I'm please and thank you ma'am
But when I've got a head full of Honkey Red
Then I don't give a good God damn.

Yes I got me a girl that I see sometimes,
She's damn near half a ton,
In a furnished room in the Joyceville pen
I got me a no-good son,
But I'll keep me a head full of Honkey Red
Until the reaper tolls the bell,
If I'm as high when I die as I was when I lived
I'll be in heaven, not in hell.
When I need a drink I'm stains on a sink
I'm please and thank you ma'am
But when I've got a head full of Honkey Red
I don't give a good God damn.

Murray McLauchlan, from his record,
Song from the Street

On the Bum in Toronto

They come to the northeast corner of Moss Park, at Shuter Street, in downtown Toronto, hoping for some kind of casual work. Maybe a truck driver needing a helper will come by, slow to a stop, inspect them, and choose one. It happens, once in a while. But not too often, as I discovered the first time I stood among the men there, the first time I was one of them. There were six or seven, standing at the curb, and another bunch, less eager, leaning against the wall. I joined the group at the curb and listened to their conversation. One was Indian, the rest white. They were talking about their last permanent jobs. A short Scottish man in his early forties, not badly dressed at all, was talking about getting laid off three months ago from his job as a shipper in a suburban warehouse. The Indian answered him with: "Hell, that ain't nothin'. I ain't had no job in two and a

half years. Up in Cochrane."

Another guy launched into a story about working for his brother-in-law and how one day the brother-in-law informed him that he was no longer needed. There is always, among the unemployed, a guy who has worked for his brother-in-law or who has a job lined up with his brother-in-law. If you're on the bum long enough you come to realize that brothers-in-law hold a very significant though obscure place in the mythology of the unemployed.

A man called Swede, a tall heavy-set man about fifty, who also didn't look all that badly off, described how for the last year he had had a good deal worked out with a certain employment agency which saw to it that he never worked less than three days a week. I gathered that he had worked an hour or two overtime with one of the agency's clients without reporting back to them. When the agency found out about it they let him go.

"Can you beat that?" the Swede said. "I work for them all that time, steady—not like some guys, you know, they get carfare in the morning and never show for the job. Buy wine with the carfare, see. I work all that time and this guy says stay for a couple hours on your own and I'll make it up to you and I do, a measly hour. And they let me go. So here I am standing on the corner."

I asked him: "How long do you usually have to wait for a truck? Couple of hours?"

"Hah!" said the Scot. "Couple days more like it!"

"For one job?"

"Yeah for one job, of maybe one hour's work."

I began hanging around the corner pretty regularly. Nothing happened for a few days, to anyone. I began to think the whole set-up was nothing more than a psychological game: you deluded yourself with the hope of work in order to keep going. Actually, I got my first job one day after I had given up. I had waited on the corner for four hours in the blistering sun and finally walked away in disgust. I walked up Sherbourne St. and crossed over to the park. I sat down on the grass and began thinking about what to do. I was broke. Then a guy in a one-ton pick-up loaded with four refrigerators stopped at the curb. The driver asked me if I wanted to earn a few dollars. The job lasted only two hours, but at least it was something.

I realized quite soon that there was a very rigid grouping of types around Moss Park. At the top of the social ladder were the most recently unemployed or laid off. These were men who had been out of work no more than, say, a month. They claimed the bench closest to Sherbourne street as their territory. They sat there, all neatly dressed, hair combed, clothes in good condition. They didn't associate with the other men and obviously felt a certain superiority. They were generally tight-lipped but if they said anything it was to let you know that their present situation was only temporary and that they had a house, kids, and *things*. Some of them were drawing union benefits and simply wanted to—needed to—add to their income. Needed to because they had possessions to pay for. You heard them continually mentioning "my car," "the house," "the TV." Their status was obvious: they were the only ones who got panhandled.

Next were the men who stood at the curb by the discount store. They had been out of work longer, but still believed their condition was temporary. Some might not have worked steadily for years, but they still actively pursued their options: waiting on the corner, visiting temporary help employment agencies, and distributing circulars.

These were the men who most vividly illustrated the contradictions, the hardships, and the unfairness in the economic situation. In them the work ethic was still thoroughly ingrained. They would work, actively *desired* work, and *needed* work. But the jobs weren't there, or if they were they went to others. These men read the papers and bristled at the news of government make-work grants. They knew the projects considered for LIP grants were organized by middle class people, usually young people, who had the information, resources and leisure with which to set up a proposal in the first place.

The third class was usually to be found just a few feet behind the men waiting at the curb. These were the guys who were lounging against the wall, hands in pockets; or sitting on the pavement, staring at their fingernails and spitting between their knees. They were in a kind of limbo. They had not yet said the hell with it and retired to benches or to lolling on the grass or to day-long bouts with the bottle; not yet. But neither did they actively look for work. When a truck slowed by the corner a shiver of activity would pass along their line. Many jumped to attention, stood up straight, even stuck out their chests. They reminded you of whores who slouch in the doorways of port cities, relaxed, and then spring to attention displaying their charms when a prospective customer hoves in sight. But the men couldn't advance the few feet to the curb and demand, with the others, to be hired. Many relaxed and sat back down again before the driver even picked anyone. An attitude of defeat, born of experience. They made the gesture mainly for themselves.

The next step, for many, is long endless days in the park broken only by the morning trek across town to the Scott Mission for food. Some don't even stir for that, although it's a good meal. If they eat at all it's probably the meagre evening meal at the Salvation Army or a fifteen-cent sandwich on Parliament street.

It's a long walk from the Sherbourne street area to the Scott Mission at Spadina and

College—long in more than distance. It can be very degrading if you still care, and for many it's just not worth it. (I can hear the refrain: "Bums, too lazy to walk a little way for their free meal. They want someone to serve it to them. And to think it's my taxes that support these loafers.") Down Queen past the Salvation Army Store, the junk shops, the temporary employment agencies with big signs demanding "REPORT AT 5 AM," the tattoo parlour, the anti-aircraft guns in front of the Armoury, Jarvis Street, old army coats and band uniforms hung up outside the corner surplus store, vacant store fronts, the restaurant which up until a year ago was owned by Chinese and served absolutely the cheapest meals in town.

You're still okay until you cross Church street. The lawn of the United Church is a buffer zone. From there on the atmosphere is hostile. Nobody pays you any attention until you start invading the business district. Picture a man, maybe forty-five, unshaven and sweaty in summer, his shoes run down, old socks unravelled at his

ankles, with baggy grease-stained trousers, a dirty shirt, perhaps a mis-matched suit jacket. He crosses Victoria street and people avert their eyes, afraid that he may say something or ask them for money. He has to pass the restaurants where shoppers are paying $1.75 for a club sandwich and businessmen sit down for pre-lunch drinks. Respectable people push him in the crowds at the corner of Yonge and nudge him closer to the curb. Eaton's and Simpson's shoppers regard him as one of the unfortunate experiences to be endured when coming downtown.

Nathan Phillips Square is the great marketplace. Bands play at lunch time, men in suits eye the secretaries' long legs dangling in the pool, teenagers eat hot dogs, and over it all you hear the slow snap of Instamatics. Henry Moore sculpture and the new luxury hotel. Through this scene walk the destitute, the down and out, the winos, the bums—panhandling here and there or lying on the grass behind the refreshment stand. Meanwhile, inside the City Hall, politicians are busy perpetuating their positions (the coming of the reformers has done nothing to decrease the number of "bums" lying on the grass with nothing to do—easily visible, easily ignored from the windows of City Hall). It is a scene the men never made and have no part of. Nathan Phillips Square is only the halfway mark and those who haven't given up continue on the hot pavements to the Scott Mission.

Time assumes a new importance when you're on the bum. Balancing a day becomes confusing if you still are trying to eat and earn some money. You have to get out of bed at 4 a.m. to be at the employment agency at 5. If you get a job at all you sometimes have to wait five hours and spend another hour getting to the job, which usually pays bare minimum. I once was sent on a job to do inventory work in a plastics factory in suburban Rexdale. I had spent three hours waiting for the call, from 6 to 9. It took me another hour or more to get to the factory. I worked from 10 until 5 and wasn't paid for a half hour lunch break—I had no money for lunch and sat watching the traffic on the highway. After taxes, I was paid eight dollars. Subtract from this the two dollars which I had to pay the agency for transportation to and from the job. I arrived back downtown at 6, and therefore had used up twelve hours of my life in order to earn six dollars. One might assume that having six dollars is a lot better than being broke. But is it? A dollar still has to come out for my one meal of the day. Further, there is the cost of a place to spend the night.

A man panhandling can actually do much better—although panhandling has proven less profitable in the past few years, due to the middle class youth from suburban high schools who come downtown in the summer and do it for sport or because it's groovy. You can see these people, the plastic generation, draped over the steps at Yonge and Wellesley, dressed in Le Chateau fashions and $30 sandals, droning "Spare change" at passersby. The curious thing is that they make money, mainly from concerned liberals who believe that they are thereby communicating with disaffected youth.

But even an old-fashioned panhandler can make something, and it's a lot easier than loading boxcars. Also, if the man's time is not taken up by work he's able to accept the free meals offered here and there. At night he can stay in the Salvation Army Hostel for men or, if he's able, he can splurge on an eighty-five-cent-a-night cot on Shuter St. He therefore makes out just as well as the man who has worked. Or better. In my opinion, his experience is less degrading because the employment agency is usually getting from the contracting company double what a worker is paid and often more.

You sometimes feel like a slave being auctioned off, but my experience in day labour hasn't been so bad—when the jobs have been available. Although I'm not in the first rank in terms of job eligibility, I make out. I have the advantages of being young and in good physical condition. I am, however, too light to be chosen for some jobs. But at least I know when somebody wants a lifter or hauler I have a *chance* of being chosen. Not so with many of the older men, their bodies ravaged by years on the bum. Also, in the eyes of potential employees every middle-aged man is a possible wino who will not show up for work at all, quit halfway through, or simply loaf the day away just to get the price of a bottle.

I've done the jobs that anyone on the bum knows: loading trucks, boats, and boxcars, driving trucks and cars, shipping, receiving, and stock taking, lifting crates and setting them down three feet away in a warehouse controlled by eight different unions. I've been a truck driver's helper a dozen times, I've swept floors, washed dishes, delivered circulars, scrubbed garbage cans for eight hours. I once ran a quarter mile so a research team could check my heart. I've painted,

mowed, raked, clipped, trimmed, dug, lifted, pushed, picked and pulled. None of these jobs lasted more than two days and none of them paid very well. Everyone else on the bum has done the same or similar jobs. I've panhandled, and I've had to steal.

Toronto unfortunately is one of the worst cities in North America to scrounge a day's work, though it ranks near the top in handing out free food and beds. Toronto is haughty. The middle class and well-to-do generally look down upon men on the bum. The prevailing view is that the best way to treat the really down and out is to ignore them. Those that have don't want to be reminded of the have-nots. It is a particularly Eastern attitude that sees poverty as some sort of affliction. On the West Coast, particularly Vancouver, Seattle, and San Francisco, the attitude is more open. There is more respect for the down and out. It has to do with tradition: the hobo, the tramp, the vagabond. Traces of an old romanticism still linger. After all, the man probably crossed an awful lot of country to get there.

Toronto is suspicious of men on the bum. One time I was flat broke but I happened to find three bus tickets on the pavement on Bay street. I began walking up Bay, trying to sell them cut rate, first at a quarter, then twenty and finally fifteen cents apiece, at every bus stop. I had to walk a long way before I could sell the three tickets. Many people seemed terrified, some looked at me with disgust. The two young junior executive types who finally bought my poor tickets did so with undisguised condescension.

In the other provinces and in Northern Ontario it's still possible to walk into a restaurant and offer your services in exchange for a meal or a dollar. I've done this elsewhere on occasions, with success, so I tried it twice in Toronto. Once I was laughed at. The other time the employees stared at me in utter disbelief.

Churches in Toronto also play a smaller role in helping the poor than elsewhere. The churches do provide a lot of charity—free coffee and sandwiches, etc.—but it's practically all directed towards transient teenagers through drop-in centres. In other parts of North America, particularly the U.S. South, you can walk into a church, claim you're a Baptist if it's Baptist, and get fixed up for a meal or a bed without any problem whatsoever. To attempt this in Toronto would be to invite a futile confrontation with the ogre of clerical bureaucracy.

So where does all this leave the man on the bum? Out on the street, where he's always been—although more so now than at any time since the 1930s. Occasionally a newspaper reporter in disguise will venture over to the Parliament street area and sleep in a flophouse or take a meal at the Scott Mission and then rush back to the office and write an "inside" story about what it's like to exist that way; occasionally you see a stray sociologist or two walking around, note pads at the ready. Poverty makes great raw material. (Professionals are forcing working people out of the area known as East of Parliament: a survey will surely reveal at least one person per block who is writing a book about the way it is in the poor part of town.) All this does for the man who is down and out is to make of him a media spectacle; just another image in the continuous montage of images fed to viewers and readers.

In truth there is nothing romantic or exotic at all about the way of life. It stinks. Those faces that—photographed in books and newspapers or flashed on a TV screen—look so experienced and wise have earned every wrinkle, every line. I've heard people comment "Gee he's really cool. He really looks like he's been around," in reference to some poor old guy trudging up Parliament. Yeah, he's been around all right, around every skid row roominghouse and bum's cafeteria in the bad part of God knows how many cities and there's no end in sight. Long after the papers have been thrown away and the images have faded, he's still out there, trudging. Trudging here for a handout, there for a lousy job, there for a filthy bed.

Maybe the poor will always be with us but the absolute down and out need not be. What perpetuates the condition is not a lack of resources but a lack of understanding, the inability to grasp the situation intuitively, the failure to realize what it means to have no future, to see nothing ahead but struggle that gets you nowhere. To know no security whatsoever, to have no family, no real friends, no culture.

You have to realize the horror of waking up at four o'clock in the morning, broke in a stinking hostel room with twenty other men, looking through the dirty window at the trash blowing down the alley, to Sherbourne street where everything is gray, and knowing you have to, you must, go out there.

Jim Christy

102

Look What's Become of Me

I seen him at Dupont and St. George,
I seen him at Spadina and Queen,
I seen him way over on Parliament street,
I'm sure that you know who I mean.
He's usually wearing a raincoat,
But never the same one for long —
And one day as I was coming out of the liquor store
He caught me and he taught me this song:

Look what's become of me,
Look what's become of me,
I was the king of New Brunswick,
Look what's become of me.

My name is George, I'm a Micmac
From down on the Miramichi,
It's been a long time since I been back.
You got a quarter for me?
Oh I was the boy to watch out for —
Ask the girls down the Miramichi,
And I can lick any man if I'm sober
Oh look what's become of me!

Look what's become of me,
Look what's become of me,
I was the king of New Brunswick,
Look what's become of me.

So I gave him a couple of quarters
'Cause that's the kind of fella I am,
I don't even know if his story was so,
And George may not even be his name,
But sometimes when I feel dejected,
Like all that I've done's come out wrong,
And I've let down my mother and father,
I remember that half-dollar song.

Look what's become of me,
Look what's become of me,
I was the king of New Brunswick,
Look what's become of me.

Bob Bossin, from the Stringband record
Thanks to the Following

The Condemned of Kaboni

For two days the medicine man danced, sang and called to the spirits of the dead. He had a problem to solve. In the 3,000-member Ojibway reserve on the eastern end of Manitoulin Island on Lake Huron, death by suicide has come with frightening frequency. In the past year, seven of thirty-eight families living in the tiny village of Kaboni have lost a son or daughter to a bullet from a .22-calibre rifle, a crudely made noose or a fistful of pills. (Another thirty-four have attempted suicide more than once.) In this one small area of farms, isolated and picturesque, the suicide rate is now ten to twenty times the national average. All of the victims were young, single and lonely. The Indians whisper about the return of the "bear walk curse," and not having their own medicine man they called one in from an American Dakotas tribe. "Why Kaboni?" they asked him. After performing his rituals he told them what he had learned: the spirits said the Indians had strayed too far from their old beliefs. That's why the young people were killing themselves.

In its own way, an inquest, called recently by local coroner Jack Bailey to look into the "epidemic" of suicides, came to the same conclusion. Sudbury psychiatrist Dr. John Ward, summoned to investigate the suicides, described the victims, all between the ages of seventeen and thirty-one, as "loners" with no self-esteem. Dependent on troubled families for support, what they found in their deteriorating homes was illness, alcoholism and poverty. "They were people with very few resources," says Ward, who also points to the cultural conflicts dividing the community—the push to be a "second-rate white man" with an education, a job and a car, and the pull to retain old values and rituals. "The suicide group tended to fall in the middle," says Ward. "They were left stranded by social conflict." The reserve is better off than most, surviving on some cattle raising and welfare, but Ward says that it is "isolation much more than poverty that causes suicides." One twenty-year-old girl left a message inked on her leg: "I hate myself—true." She also left a note for a nonexistent lover.

The inquest's all-Indian jury made a number of recommendations, now slowly being implemented. It asked the appropriate governments for more counsellors to help broken families (there is only one counsellor on the reserve now). It asked for recreational facilities for a community where the main distractions are

drinking and fighting. It asked for a home for troubled children and a mental health clinic. But mostly it asked for ways to revive Indian culture, especially at the high-school level. Indian children leaving grade school are bused as much as sixty miles to a big modern, school which serves all native and white students on Manitoulin Island. Among native children absenteeism is common and the dropout rate high, the result of "culture shock" at meeting the outside world for the first time, says Indian high-school trustee Alex Fox. Adds a former teacher, Mary-Lou Fox, herself an Indian: "The kids never really learn anything about being Indian. The school is supposed to be an extension of the home, but it isn't."

Skepticism persists among the Indians of Kaboni that such changes will stop the suicides. Some of them say the deaths were inevitable, that they had a certain dignity. The Indians regarded the inquest as "an intrusion into a private personal tragedy," says coroner Bailey, a general practitioner in Little Current, the island's main town. Now that the medicine man has come and gone, says Alex Fox, "we know a little what is wrong, what we must do, and we'll take care of it." But the fear of the bear walk curse remains. It first came to the attention of outsiders about twenty years ago when an Indian accused of killing his father blamed his actions on the "bear walk." Many Indians believe that if a medicine man places the curse on an individual or family, it can cause illness, abnormal actions or misfortune. One native studies expert says the name comes from the fact that victims are believed to take on a bear-like gait.

Gabriel Aibens has lost two of his nine children to suicide—one of them just hours after the inquest ended. Aibens is a Roman Catholic and will not talk of the possibility of a medicine man's curse. "God will take people away and there's not too much people can do. It's beyond our power." Aibens himself has had both his legs amputated because of a blood disease, so he sits in a wheelchair, apart from a television set, the only new and bright object in the two-room shack that is his home. "The bad things happening seem to be a month apart," he says in Ojibway to a counsellor. "Either an accident or a suicide. I guess it will happen again. If anybody could stop it, they should try."

Twenty-four-year-old Simon Aibens was the first to go on November 1. He had been drinking

heavily when in the middle of the night he went into a bedroom where his sister and two children were sleeping and shot himself. He had talked of a premonition and given away his television set in preparation for death. "It was a definite thing," says his father. "There didn't seem to be anything we could do about it." Phillip Aibens, twenty-seven, took an overdose of pills one and a half months later. But the father doesn't think too much about the dead. He has the living to worry about. His twenty-two-year-old daughter Shirley, an unmarried mother, is in psychiatric hospital after attempting suicide. Another son is dropping out of school.

The real curse afflicting the Indians of Manitoulin Island is, as the medicine man and the Sudbury psychiatrist seemed to agree, lack of identity. Young Indians on this reserve, as in many others, are finding that without self-respect they can't function in a white man's world. Worse, they can no longer function in their own. After years of watching their language deteriorate and their parents chasing the white man's dreams, the young are looking for ways to go back. "What they see in the white man's world, they don't value," says Alex Fox. "But it's not enough just to say, 'I'm Indian.' The culture must be imbedded in us. Otherwise, we will be disoriented." And, he might have added, the suicides will continue to devastate in Kaboni.

Angela Ferrante, *Maclean's*

When the white man came we had the land and they had the bibles; now they have the land and we have the bibles.

Chief Dan George

The federal government has told the McPherson people that they want to create a national historic site here. They propose to put up a plaque telling some of the important history of this area. As you know, my people have lived in this area for thousands of years and there are many events that are worthy of recognition. There are many Indian heroes and many examples of courage and dedication to the people. We have a rich and proud history.

But what events does the federal government consider history? Let me read you the text that they propose for the plaque. It is in both English and French, but I will read you the English.

In 1840 John Bell of the Hudson Bay Company built the first Fort McPherson four miles upriver from here. Moved to this site in 1848, it was for over fifty years the principal trading post in the Mackenzie Delta region and, after 1860, a centre of missionary activity. In 1903 Inspector Charles Constantine established the first R.N.W.M.P. post in the Western Arctic here. In the winter of 1898-99 a number of overlanders tried to use Fort McPherson as a base to reach the Klondike.

Where are we mentioned on this plaque, Mr. Berger? Where is there mention of any of our history? The history of the Peel River people did not begin in 1840. We have been here for a long time before that, yet we get no mention. Does the federal government not consider us to be human too? Do they think that we don't make history?

Richard Nerysoo, from *The Past and Future Land*, by Martin O'Malley

Potlatch

The problem, as every member of the acquisitive society will have noticed by now, is not in amassing things but in getting rid of them. Look into your closets, O Western World, and you will see a rising flood of things threatening to engulf you—a surfeit of all the fair and flagrant things that human and mechanical ingenuity can devise. One acquires them as desiderata; afterward, many of them turn out to be things that the department of sanitation cannot be prevailed upon to haul away. Sometimes, by happy chance, one can manage to lose things, and three moves are as good as a fire, as my New England grandmother used to say. But a far more stylish way of disposing of a lot of things in a hurry is the time-honoured northwest coast Indian potlatch. In the midst of our great crisis of the Malthusian supermarket a study of the ways of the potlatchers can teach us something.

The Indians of the Pacific coast used to be very good at making things, and they produced vast quantities of them, for they lived in a region where the salmon and halibut were so thick they did everything but catch themselves. That left the human population with time on their hands for

making spruceroot rain hats, mountain-sheep horn spoons, cedarwood boxes inlaid with haliotis shell and snail opercula, argillite grease-dishes, maplewood soapberry-beating paddles, blankets of mountain-goat hair and cedar bark, whale's-tooth amulets, and such.

Since arts and crafts (and, to a lesser extent, sex) were the Indians' main preoccupation before the white man introduced liquor, money, and book-keeping, their longhouses would periodically fill to overflowing with the results of everybody's incessant basket weaving, wood carving, and stone chiselling. But to keep these from becoming a burden on the tribal psyche, their chief would hold a potlatch and give everything away in one great orgy of generosity. Potlatches were given to celebrate the accession of a new chief, the raising of a totem pole, the assumption of a crest or title, and so on; the word derives from the Nootka patshatl, "to give". If the potlatching chief impoverished himself and his clan in the process, so much the better, for by his very lavishness he acquired an unpurchasable esteem in the community. Besides, custom dictated that the recipients of his gifts must go him one better at their next potlatch.

A proper potlatch involved prodigious displays of eating, since it was a point of honour with the host to provide much more food than his guests could consume. The eating would last for days, interspersed with singing, belching, speechmaking, dramatic performances, and the ceremonial conferring of honorific names. But the vital part of the occasion was the bestowing of gifts—bowls, boxes, baskets, blankets, canoes, ornaments, sculptures—that the chief had collected among his people, from each according to his ability, and now distributed among his guests, to each according to his rank.

Potlatching replaced warfare and violence as a way of settling tribal disputes after the Canadian and United States governments began asserting their authority along the coast. "When I was young I saw a stream of blood shed in war," said an old Kwakiutl in a speech in 1895. "But since that time the white men came and stopped up that stream of blood with wealth. Now we fight with our wealth."

The Hudson's Bay Company's factory-made blankets replaced deerskin and mountain-goat robes just at the time when potlatching reached new heights of conspicuous consumption, having been accelerated by the tribal chiefs' need to assert their prerogatives in a rapidly changing world. A chief grown wealthy in the fur trade would demonstrate his contempt for property by giving away and destroying whole households—burning canoes, clubbing slaves to death, and breaking his most valuable "coppers" in the process. The coppers—shaped like shields and decorated with totemic figures—were, in effect, bills of high denomination that enabled a chief to get rid of a great deal of wealth at one go. Often they were worth more than their weight in gold, for they had the disconcerting habit of doubling their value every time they changed hands; and it was not uncommon for a copper to be worth ten or fifteen thousand trade blankets.

To be able to break so powerful a copper before an audience of one's invited rivals was a tremendous honour. But the game was usually rigged, since the broken pieces could be picked up and either resold at a profit or used to embarrass a neighbour. "A chief may break his copper and give the broken parts to his rival," explains the pioneer anthropologist Franz Boas, who watched a lot of potlatching before the turn of the century. "If the latter wants to keep his prestige, he must

break a copper of equal or higher value, then return both his own broken copper and the fragments which he received. . . ."

Later, when coppers went out of circulation, the potlatch people shifted to trade goods and introduced a whole department-store repertory to take their place. The Kwakiutl chief Daniel Cranmer drew up a partial inventory for the anthropologist Dr. Helen Codere when he described a memorable potlatch he held at Village Island, British Columbia, in 1921: "I gave him [the chief of nearby Cape Mudge village] a gas boat and $50 cash. Altogether that was worth $500 . . . The same day I gave Hudson's Bay blankets. I started giving out the property. First the canoes. Two pool tables were given to two chiefs. It hurt them. They said it was the same as breaking a copper. The pool tables were worth $350 apiece. Then bracelets, gas lights, violins, guitars were given to the more important people. Then twenty-four canoes, some of them big ones, and four gas boats." Later he handed out jewellery, shawls, sweaters, and shirts for women and young people; button blankets, shawls and 400 trade blankets; washtubs, teapots, cups, and about 1,000 washbasins. Handfuls of small change were flung to the children. "The fourth day I gave away furniture: boxes, trunks, sewing machines, gramophones, bedsteads and bureaus. The fifth day I gave away cash. The sixth day I gave away about 1,000 sacks of flour worth $3 a sack. I also gave sugar." When it was over, he was unchallengeably one up on every other chief in the region. "All the chiefs say now in a gathering, 'You cannot expect that we can ever get up to you. You are a great mountain'."

Potlatches of a sort are still given occasionally in the northwest coast Indian country, but nowadays the institution retains only a faint glimmer of its former magnificence. Since they no longer have art objects to give away, they simply throw parties at which everybody receives . . . money. The end is clearly in sight. The white man has never shown much understanding for the potlatch; it was outlawed by the Canadian government, and even sympathetic anthropologists have described it as an "atrocious" and "paranoid" pursuit of social prestige. Most of them have missed the point; namely, that potlatching was essentially a primitive, preliterate form of investment banking.

From an economist's standpoint the wealthy

Indian chief accomplished the same results by ostensibly giving things away as does the modern millionaire by supposedly holding on to them. In our paper economy the millionaire doesn't keep his wealth around the house, either—except for a Modigliani or two. What he doesn't need for his personal consumption he gives to a bank, in the form of pieces of power-paper inscribed with totems. The bank, in turn, ladles it out to the economy as a whole in the form of loans. The main thing is that people (beginning with the bank manager) must know that the money, though invisible, is actually there. It is this knowledge that determines a man's status as a millionaire;

otherwise he's just a Collyer brother hoarding rubbish.

A Kwakiutl chief, depositing his wealth with his rivals, also depended on that public knowledge for his power, though he never had to worry about bankruptcies or a drop in the price of coppers. At the highest level, the cycle of acquisition and distribution is virtually identical in both cases. If our millionaire is very, very rich, social pressure and the tax structure will induce him, sooner or later, to do some heavy potlatching of the modern sort: the name of the game is Rockefeller Foundation.

Frederic V. Grunfeld

Destroying A Nation

Mr. Berger, my name is Phillip Blake and I am a Treaty Indian from Fort McPherson. I have worked as a social worker here in Fort McPherson for the past five and a half years.

First, I would like to say I am not an old man, but I have seen many changes in my life. Fifteen years ago, most of what you see as Fort McPherson did not exist. Take a look around the community now and you will start to get an idea of what has happened to the Indian people here over the past few years.

Look at the housing where transient government staff live. And look at the housing where the Indian people live. Look at how the school and hostel, the RCMP and Government staff houses are right in the centre of town, dividing the Indian people into two sides. Look at where the Bay store is, right on top of the highest point of land. Mr. Berger, do you think that that is the way the Indian people chose to have this community? Do you think the people here had any voice in planning the community? Do you think they would have planned it so that it would divide them? Do you think they would have planned it so that it divided them and gave them a poorer standard than the transient whites who come in, supposedly to help them?

Take a look at the school here. Try to find anything that makes it a place where Indian values, traditions and Indian culture is respected. It could be a school in the suburbs of Edmonton, Toronto or Vancouver. Do you think Indian people would have chosen a building like this as a way to teach their children how to be proud of their Indian heritage? Do you think Indian people chose to have their children taught that the only way to survive in the future is to become like the white man?

Look around you. Look at this building. Find out who the teachers are. Find out what they teach our children. Find out what regulations there are in this school. Find out who decides these regulations, who hires the teachers and who fires them.

The school is just a symbol of white domination and control. It is a part of a system set up to destroy Indian culture and to destroy our pride in our Indian heritage. It is only part of that system. Look at some of the other parts. Do you think people chose to live in rental houses owned by the government instead of in houses they built for themselves and owned by themselves? Do you think they chose to have a system of justice which

often they can not understand and which does not allow them to help their own people and deal with their own problems? A system which punishes the Indians for stealing from the Bay, but does not punish the Bay for stealing from the Indians?

Do you think that they chose to become cheap labour for oil companies, construction companies and government, instead of working for themselves and developing their own economy, in their own way?

In short, Mr. Berger, can you or anyone else really believe that we Indian people are now living the way we have chosen to live? Can you really believe that we have chosen to have high rates of alcoholism, murder, suicide and social breakdown? Do you think we have chosen to become beggars in our own homeland?

Mr. Berger, you are well aware that hundreds of years ago, in southern Canada and in the United States, many Indian civilizations were destroyed. In some cases, this was done simply by killing off the Indian people who occupied the land, the land that was valuable to white settlers. In other cases, it was done by restricting the Indians to small reserves where they could no longer hunt, fish and make a living from their land. In all cases, it was pretty clear that whatever the white man wanted, the white man got. When he wanted greater land for farming, he cleared off the trees and he cleared off the Indians. When he wanted to dig the gold or minerals from the land, he killed the Indians who tried to defend their land.

In James Bay, when the white man decided that he wanted to again play God and change the course of mighty rivers so he could make money and power from them, he corralled the Indian people into reserves and flooded the Indian land. The nations of Indians and Eskimos in the north had been slightly luckier.

For a while it seemed that we might escape the greed of the southern system. The north was seen as a frozen wasteland, not fit for the civilized ways of the white man; but that has been changing over the past few years. Now the system of genocide practiced on our Indian brothers in the south over the past few hundred years is being turned loose on us and our Eskimo brothers. "Don't be silly," you may say, "we are sorry about what we did in the past; we made some mistakes, but it's different now. Look, we give you an education, houses and health services." Mr. Berger, the system of genocide may have become a little more polished over the past few hundred years in order to suit the civilized tastes of the southern people who watch Lloyd Robertson on "The National", but the effect is exactly the same.

We are being destroyed. Your nation is destroying our nation. What we are saying today, here and now, is exactly what Louis Riel was saying roughly a hundred years ago. We are a nation. We have our own land, our own ways, and our own civilization. We do not want to destroy you or your land. Please do not destroy us. You and I both know what happened to Louis Riel. Yet now, a hundred years later, your Prime Minister is willing to say that Louis Riel was not all wrong. He is willing to *say* that, a hundred years later, but is he willing to change the approach that destroyed Louis Riel? And his nation? And is now threatening to destroy us?

I am sure that throughout your visits to native communities, Mr. Berger, you have been shown much of the hospitality that is our tradition. We have always tried to treat our guests well; it never occurred to us that our guests would one day claim that they owned our whole house. Yet that is what is happening.

White people came as visitors to our land. Suddenly, they claim it as their land. They claim that we have no right to call it Indian land—land that we have occupied and used for thousands of years, which just recently the white man has come to visit. Is this the great system of justice which your nation is so proud of?

Now look at what happened to France during the Second World War. Germany moved in and occupied the land that France claimed as her own.

At that time, Canada seemed willing to help a people whose land had been unjustly taken. Now, the same thing is happening to Indian nations of the north. Your nation has suddenly decided to move in and occupy land that is rightfully ours.

Where is your great tradition of justice today? Does your nation's greed for oil and gas suddenly override justice? What exactly is your superior civilization that can so blindly ignore the injustice which occurs continually over one-third of the land-mass in Canada and yet which barely gets reported on your TV or in your newspapers?

One-third of the land mass of Canada is under direct colonial rule. Yet you seem willing to talk only of igloos, polar bears and snow when you talk about the north. One has to read about South Africa or Rhodesia to get a clear picture of what is really happening in northern Canada. While your newspapers and television talk about sports fishing up here, we as a people are being destroyed. It doesn't even merit any coverage.

Look at us, and what we stand for, before you accept without further thought that the Indian nation must die. In many parts of the world people are starving. It is said that two-thirds of the people of the world go to bed hungry each night. We Indian people are sometimes accused of not being willing to share our resources, but what of this absurd scheme that Arctic Gas has dreamt up? What does it offer to those who are starving? Does it promise to use our resources and our land to help those who are poor? It suggests exactly the opposite.

It suggests that we give up our land and our resources to the richest nation in the world, not the poorest. We are threatened with genocide only so that the rich and the powerful can become more rich and more powerful. Mr. Berger, I suggest that in any man's view, that is immoral. If our Indian nation is being destroyed so that poor people of the world might get a chance to share this world's riches, then as Indian people I am sure that we would seriously consider giving up our resources.

But do you really expect us to give up our life, our lands, so that those few people who are the richest and the most powerful in the world can maintain and defend their immoral position of privilege? That is not our way. I strongly believe that we do have something to offer your nation, something other than our minerals. I believe it is in the self-interest of your own nation to allow the

Indian nation to survive and develop in our own way, on our own land. For thousands of years, we have lived with our land; we have taken care of the land, and the land has taken care of us. We did not believe that our society had to grow and to expand and conquer new areas in order that we could fulfill our destiny as Indian people.

We have lived with the land, not tried to conquer or control it, or rob it of its riches. That is not our way. We have not tried to get more and more riches and power; we have not tried to conquer new frontiers or outdo our parents or make sure that every year we are richer than the year before.

We have been satisfied to see our wealth as ourselves and the land we live with. It is our greatest wish to be able to pass this on, this land, to succeeding generations in the same condition that our fathers have given it to us. We have not tried to improve the land and we have not tried to destroy it. That is not our way.

I believe that your nation might wish to see us, not as a relic from the past, but as a way of life, a system of values by which you might survive. We do not wish to push our world onto you, but we are willing to defend it for ourselves, our children and our grandchildren. If your nation becomes so violent that it would tear up our land, destroy our society and our future and occupy our homeland by trying to impose this pipeline against our will, then we will have no choice but to react with violence. I hope we do not have to do that, for it is not the way we would choose.

However, if we are forced to blow up the pipeline, I hope you will not only look on the violence of Indian action, but also on the violence of your own nation which would force us to take such a course. We will never initiate violence but, if your nation threatens by its own violent action to destroy our nation, you will have given us no choice.

Please do not force us into this position, for we would all lose too much.

Mr. Berger, I believe it is because I am a social worker here that I have had to make some sense out of the frustration and desperation that people in this community and others along the valley are feeling. It is clear to me that the pipeline in Alaska has not been any part of progress, whatever progress may mean. Where progress should mean people getting greater control over their own lives, greater freedom, the pipeline in

Alaska appears to have driven people into the ground, along with the pipeline.

Mr. Berger, it should be very clear by now what the wishes are of the people along the Mackenzie Valley. If we lived in any kind of democratic system, there would be no further talk of an Arctic Gas pipeline. The will of the people has been made clear. If this consensus, if the will of the people is not respected, then I appeal to you and all people of southern Canada to respect and support us in our efforts to re-establish democracy and democratic decision-making in our homeland.

I guess the question for southern Canada is simply, which side are you on? Are you on the side of the people trying to find freedom and a democratic tradition? Or are you on the side of those who are trying to frustrate our attempts to find freedom and who are instead trying to destroy the last free Indian nation?

Mr. Berger, I guess what I am really trying to say is, can you help us? And can we help you make sure that the will of the people is respected? After all, isn't this supposed to be what Canada once stood for? Can we as an Indian nation help Canada to once again become a true democracy?

Phillip Blake, from *The Past and Future Land*, by Martin O'Malley

Land ought not to be a commodity, because like air and water it is necessary to human existence; and all men have by birthright equal rights to its use.

Phillips Thompson

My Little Indian

Hee haw, hee haw. That's a horse laugh. I didn't suffer during the thirties and I had a damn good time and there wasn't much I couldn't do and I always had me a good horse and a woman and booze and I lived by my wits, just a poor but smart sailor boy from Iowa. I seen a lot of the world and in, oh, 1932, I got into a fight in a bar in San Francisco and pounded a guy half to death and a couple more punches and it would have been the marble orchard for him. I could hit. With my crime sheet and then this, well there was no way I wasn't going to be behind bars for a long time and believe me, in them days, a navy brig was worse than any Siberia. I headed for Canada and stole a truck at Everett and slipped across the border on a back road at night and I puttered along into New Westminister and went into a used car lot and picked out the oldest wreck I could see and undid the license plates. You see what I'm getting at. The U.S. Navy teaches you a thing or two. Or three. Then I put those plates on my pickup and threw the Washington state ones in the river. So I had a Canadian truck with Canadian papers, from the old wreck, understand, and they were good enough that I sold the truck for $260 in Mission. It was a good truck. I also sold a box of tools that were in the cab of the truck so I had a stake of about $275, plus what was left of my navy pay after buying clothes after I took off from that bar.

I caught a bus up to the Cariboo, Jesus Christ, what a ride, and I bought a horse at Clinton and a saddle and a bit of an outfit and rode around the hills a week learning to ride that horse. It was a brown gelding and it had it in for me every morning, every day for five years. Many a stick I broke on him. My first job was with a good guy named Marriott in that country and he knew I was no hand but he gave me a job that summer and I spent it nursemaiding calves and figuring how I could beat the system. That fall after work was done this guy, Marriott, asked me to stay on, no money, but room and board, and I said no.

He didn't know it but his count was three short because I'd driven three of his steers up into the hills and so there was no brand and I had three pretty good animals going for me. I rode out of his place in October, first snow was flying, with $27 for three months work, and I circled back and loaded up my horse with a couple of axes, two saws, a file, gunny sacks, candles, a lantern, plane, chisels, sledge, a lot of stuff I'd swiped, worth no more, I'd say, than twenty bucks. Added to the wages and the three young ones, it made a decent summer's wages in the style to which I had become accustomed. U.S. Navy.

I bought a pack horse for five bucks and loaded her up and headed across to the country over against the Fraser River and I got a woman, too. Just rode into an Indian camp and made a deal with her old man. Louise, a pretty fine woman, a girl then. For ten dollars and one steer, and she brought her own pony, an Indian pony that would go forever. The old man had a Winchester 44-40 and I bought that for ten, I think he skinned me on it, but he threw in a box of shells. I told Louise to bring along anything she owned but did you ever see an Indian girl with a hope chest? Ha! Ha! She had some blankets, some clothes, a skinning knife, a honey pail full of pretty rocks she'd gathered for years in the creek, and some of those small pamphlets which the missionaries, the priests, gave out with the covers showing God and Jesus floating up there in the sky. The first night we used one to light the fire and my little squaw laughed like hell. Laughed and laughed. So much for religion in the Woods' household.

We went back in the hills and found a trapper's cabin in good shape and I patched up the stove and put some shakes on the roof and we both worked like hell, me on the north end of the axe and she dragging the poles with the gelding to the cabin, and we got in our wood and then we had to decide what to do with the steers. You see, we had no hay, and horses can winter in that country, but cows just can't. They can't scrape through the snow crust to the grass below. Louise knew what to do. You know what she did? She just walked over with the knife and she put her hand just above the tail and ran it along the backbone and when she got to the steer's neck, snick, in went the knife and the beast never knew it was dead. Then I knew I had me a real woman.

There was none of this steak for breakfast, lunch and dinner. No sir. She butchered them down to the last ounce and every bit of fat, and she made jerky and she made pemmican. You grind up the jerky and put in berries, anything to give it flavor, like raisins, and you mix it up with tallow and store it in airtight bags of leather, and you take a pound of that pemmican into the bush on a thirty below day and it will keep you going forever.

She was quite a gal, and remember she was only fifteen, and she loved her white man with the tattoo on his arm. She used to study it for minutes at a time and talk to herself in the Indian tongue and I never knew what she meant.

There was the odd moose to the north of us and she could find them, she knew where their yarding-up places would be although she'd never been there. Some Indians know these things. They say an Indian has to be taught to live in the bush just like a white man, but this is just not so.

She helped me a lot, that little girl. I began thinking like an Indian and she like a white man and we got along fine. We lived together for four years and in the summer I went cowboying and she would work in the The Lake (*Williams Lake*) or somewhere, and we were both stealing them all blind. Our cabin back of Big Creek was getting to be a fine place, a garden in the spring which didn't seem to grow weeds and we had corn and spuds and pumpkins in the fall and I guess we lived on about $200 a year cash money. Two hundred a year, and that included giving pretty good Christmas presents to her folks. The old Winchester always got us a moose. God! It threw a slug that would stop a freight train. We had fool hen and plenty of fish and some vegetables and we bought sugar and flour and salt and beans and kerosene and grease, cloth, latigo, some oats for the horses and a crock of hootch for Christmas and we made an awful lot of stuff and I taught her to read and write and she taught me the bush.

No, no kids. They just never seemed to come along.

Once the B.C. police came up, and they seemed awful curious and Louise fed them a big moose steak, out of season, of course, and I always bought a steer from a rancher each fall and got a bill of sale so we ate beef and deer and moose all year on that one bill of sale and usually it was a beef that Louise had given the old treatment to. The friendly voice, the hand on the backbone and the creature would just wait for the knife.

She made me vests and chaps out of leather and she kept the place clean and she put up magazine pictures on the walls and even kept flowers in winter. Red geraniums. I'll never see a geranium but what I'll remember my little Indian. I'd say we lived four years on less then $800, from haying, a bit of cowboying and Louise sold a few vests and jackets of deerskin and coyotes in winter prime, beginning in November, got a good price of about eight or ten dollars with the trader, so we did okay.

Of course, it wasn't all peaches and cream, not that we ever saw cream. Or peaches either. Louise gave me some trouble but not because she was Indian. Because she was a woman. Those pictures on the walls. The lady magazine things. Out there, goddammit, was another world. Shiny cars and long dresses and champagne. Why couldn't we go out to Vancouver? Let's go to Vancouver. Woodsy? When we going to see Vancouver and the moving shows? I told her that outside there, the whole world was going belly up.

It was the Dirty Thirties, of course, but here was a girl nineteen, as pretty as a mountain lily, tall and slim and smart, and she had never seen a moving show or heard a radio or worn a right dress and, well, for Christ's sakes, it was only a matter of time before I caved in. So one morning I said, "Okay, get your gear together. We'll ride over to Clinton and catch the PGE (*The Pacific Great Eastern Railway*) and we'll go down to town. Vancouver." She was like a kid with a new red wagon. I had a mind to steal a car, pull the old used car lot plate switch, rustle up some money any way I could, and I had a few ideas. Not a very nice fellow, am I? Well, no, I'm not. Anyway, we were going to live and love it up and no bullshit about it.

Three days later we closed her up and I went and saddled the horses and if you don't believe me, then to hell with you, but when I brought them around there she was standing by the door in an outfit I couldn't believe. It was high society you'd call it, just like the smart city outfits in the magazines and she'd somehow bought the material, the fall before, I guess, and studied the pictures and made these clothes, hat, jacket, skirt, blouse, the works. Her feet were still in moccasins.

Well, I oohed and awed and she giggled and we started down the trail and she was sidesaddle, the skirt you see. Sidesaddle on a western saddle, if you want to believe it. Ladylike as hell. We came to the first creek and her pinto, one of those Indian scrub, he must have caught an eye just then, a flash of her red skirt. Red, hell, it was scarlet. He gave a sideways jump, more of a skitter, but Louise was sidesaddle and that was enough and off she went, sort of tumbling, not sliding, and I heard this crack. A distinct crack. Her head had hit a rock in the stream. Somehow, something told me she was dead before I got to her. She was. Not even a smile for me at the end. Just dead. I tied her in the saddle and went on leading her pony and her Dad's place, you'll remember, was about twenty miles down the road and we got there before dark and next morning we buried her in her pink and scarlet city clothes by some pretty poplars, out of sight.

We didn't need no priest. We didn't even think of one. It was me and Louise and the rest of the world, all your goddamned records and social security cards and car insurance cards and names in a big census book in Ottawa didn't exist. It was just me and her people buried her in a board casket and I stood at the head of the grave as her brothers and cousins dumped in the soil and I said, "Goodbye, Louise, I loved you, and I'm glad you didn't see the city." I told her people I wouldn't be back and the cabin and everything in it was for them, and the brother Manuel said he was going to put a white cross on the grave and he'd send me a painting of it if he knew where I was going to be and I said I didn't know where I was going to be and I got on my gelding, the same one I'd rode into that country on and seen Louise, and I got on the horse and I rode out of that goddamned country and I never went back. (*He breaks down and cries.*)

as told to Barry Broadfoot, in *Ten Lost Years*

Ol Antoine

She fed young John his bottle and kept him quiet. From time to time she went to the window to peer out through a small hole burred through the frost that covered the panes. The cabin was beginning to creak in the chill of the gathering night when she spotted Ol Antoine coming up the path from the old soddie cabin. Then she reached the table in three long steps, put her face opposite his on the table and said in a tight and hard voice, "Smith!"

His head came up. He was instantly, fully awake. It was a peculiar ability of his that often startled her. Now, looking into his dark eyes, the pupil unclearly separated from the iris, the look flat and dull as a piece of cloth, she wondered again if there were Indian blood in Smith. So many of the old families had Indian blood.

He waited for her to speak.

"Ol Antoine is coming up here", she said. "He's been down in that old soddie cabin in the sidehill."

"Well, that is nothing to get excited about, except maybe for me, as he has finally come to break that quarter horse for me, I s'pose. I was thinkin' today that by God . . ."

She broke in. "Never mind about that stupid horse. I tell you I have been scared witless for two days."

"Scared? Of Ol Antoine?"

She lowered her voice. "There is somebody in there with him", she said.

"Aah", said Smith, speaking as one to whom all things have at last become clear, "someone with him. I tell you, it is a girl. That's what it is. It is a girl. It's a love nest he's got down there. Let me see now, how old is Ol Antoine? I once added up all the stories he's told about himself and I think it came out to one hundred and thirty-four—and that would be three years ago—so he'd be a hundred thirty-seven. . . ."

"This is no joke, Smith, and it is no girl in that old soddie."

"Of course it is a girl, and a good thing, too. It is a great opportunity for me. Now, while he is inflamed with passion, at the age of a hundred and thirty-seven, now I am at last in a good position to make sure he finally does that job for me." He rose from the table. "Yes sir, he is going to do that job this year, and no mistake about it."

Before she could answer the door opened slowly and Ol Antoine said "Hello, this place."

"Why," said Smith, "if it ain't Ol Antoine. Klahowya, old man." He then turned to Norah and, speaking loudly, said, "It is the turn of the Smith luck, Norah. This winter ain't gonna be known any more as the Smith Disaster. Ol Antoine has come to break that quarter horse for me."

The old man looked at him and then walked out of the kitchen, past the ladder-like stairs that led to the bedrooms and into the sitting-room. There he seated himself beside the drum heater. It was a small room, but it contained many deer horns, sheep horns, moose horns and guns; also reproduction of Remington and Russell prints; photographs of horses, homemade copper bas-reliefs of horses' heads, an escritoire jammed with unopened bills and unanswered letters, and a chesterfield and an arm chair with broken springs. Ol Antoine did not use a chair. He upended a piece of firewood and sat on it.

Smith leaned in the doorway, watching him and ignoring Norah, who was plucking at his sleeve. Smith liked to look at Ol Antoine. He could never fully understand what was in the old Indian's mind, and he respected that in any man.

Ol Antoine was an interesting sight, by normal standards. He had heaped upon himself all the thin clothing that he owned. His feet were in ankle-length moccasins, over which he had drawn thin dress rubbers. His pants were of heavy blue serge. They had been obtained somehow through a used clothing outlet and were now shiny with the fat of many beaver skinnings.

Ol Antoine's sweater had been knitted by a member of some women's auxiliary to something, possibly for the benefit of the troops at Sebastopol. On his head was a black hat, which he did not remove. Around his ears was wound a scarf. This old man was variously described as uncle, grandfather, great-grandfather and, of course, cousin by most of the Indians on the Namko Reserve. His true age was a matter of speculation, even for those interested enough to consider it. The first whites to take up land in the Namko Country remembered him as being exceptionally tall, but now he was less than five-five; the gristle separating his vertebrae had thinned and granulated, the normal S curve of the spine had become exaggerated and his head was now carried low on his thin neck. Some said Ol Antoine would never die, in the ordinary sense, but would one day just disappear in a puff of his own dust. He was a man possessed of many stories, rarely told. It was said that he claimed to have ridden with Chief Joseph of the Nez Percés when that nation fought the American cavalry regiments in its long and unsuccessful attempt to get over the Canadian border, seeking the haven that Canada had not long before given to Sitting Bull and his Sioux. It would be possible, were Ol Antoine over ninety now and under twenty during the Nez Percé war, that he did take part in that sad campaign, but highly improbable. The Chilcotin language bears about as much relationship to the Nez Percés' as does Chinese to Dutch and in any case the Chilcotins were a lonely group of Indians who kept aloof from even the neighbouring Shuswap across the Fraser River.

They were a people noted for high cheekbones, wide mouths and sultry temperament. In 1864 they had carried out a small war against the whites. Their leader had been a big man with a wide mouth and hard mind whose name comes down as Klatsassan-Chilhoseltz. Klatsassan had blue eyes, which might be taken as a tribute to the warrior spirit of visiting Caucasians,

although it is a curious fact that the first white man ever known to pass through the Chilcotin, Sir Alexander Mackenzie, noted in his diary that he was met by blue-eyed Indians somewhere south of the West Road River. Possibly Cossack blood from the Russian steppes had filtered through Alaska and into Chilcotin before Mackenzie's time.

The British Columbia colonial government had listed the uprising as a war, seeking to be repaid for the costs of its volunteer soldiers by the Colonial Office in London. This failed and the uprising later came to be called the Waddington Massacre and was dismissed from public notice as just another brawl. It was forgotten by almost everybody, except a few Chilcotins.

Ol Antoine claimed to have been a warrior for the Chilcotins also, but then he claimed so many things.

The Chilcotins are the southernmost extension of the great mass of Athapaskan-speaking Indians who cover the north of Canada. Islands of people who speak a related language extend far to the south and into modern Mexico. In the United States the best-known members of this group are the Navahoes and Apaches, who were similarly dissatisfied when whites took their land away from them.

Interestingly enough, in the centre of the modern Navaho Reservation, north of Gallup, New Mexico, is a lonely butte, which geographers call Ship Rock but which is, according to Navaho legend, the Great Bird that brought their ancestors down from the north.

After killing a few whites and dodging two small white armies, Klatsassan and some of his fellows surrendered. The government temporarily suspended war status and treated them as murder suspects instead of as prisoners of war, and they went on trial before Mr. Justice Begbie.

(It might be said that their defence was conducted under some handicap, since the evidence of wild Indians was not then accepted in British Columbia courts. This, however, was later rectified and the present B.C. Evidence Act (Section 12, Chapter 134, Revised Statutes of British Columbia, 1960) provides that a judge may receive "evidence of any aboriginal native, or native of mixed blood of the continent of North America, or the islands adjacent thereto, being an uncivilized person, destitute of knowledge of God and of any fixed and clear belief in religion or in a future state of rewards and punishments, without

118

administering oath. . . . ")

On October twenty-sixth that year Klatsassan, Taloot, Tapeet, Chessus and young Pierre were all taken out and hanged together at Quesnelmouth.

Klatsassan left few words and little mark upon his country. The only legend which comes down from that campaign is that when he surrendered in the expectation of pardon and was ordered to give up his musket he broke it against a tree instead and said, "King George man big liar." But there is no proof of this and it is believed, generally, only by the Chilcotins.

It was, in any event, of no concern to Smith on this cold evening. If he had ever heard such tales, they had failed to impress him. His only apparent interest on this day was the quarter horse, and he began by discussing that animal.

"It is maybe going to take us a day or two to round up that horse, Ol Antoine," he said. Ol Antoine did not answer.

Smith twisted a cigarette for the old man and continued speaking, gently, as he did so.

"I come all the way down the Home Place Meadow today without spotting him. He must be off with the half-wild bunch of mine that hang out on Happy Ann Meadow. We tried to bring him into the ranch yard so he might gentle up some but every time he went out right over the fence. He is like a deer now."

Ol Antoine spoke in his own language to an audience that one might judge to be larger and more distant than Smith. Smith touched his arm to restore Ol Antoine's attention and held the cigarette before him. Ol Antoine took it, held it between his thumb and middle finger, allowed Smith to light it for him and then, pushing his lips out to meet the cigarette as his hand brought it back towards his mouth, he puffed smoke rapidly without inhaling. He did not smoke often.

"You know, Ol Antoine, there are people who would say that you are a little bit late in breaking that horse for me, on account of that horse has now passed his sixth birthday and has never felt the touch of leather."

Ol Antoine lifted one arm and spoke slowly, but with feeling, to a band council or to some other group of people who understood Chilcotin.

"Who cares about that damn horse?" said Norah.

"I care," said Smith. "That is going to be a great horse. A really great horse."

"It is Bulldog Quarter Horse, and you know it. Look at how heavy them shoulders are, look at

them pasterns, it'll have a trot that will jar your head off."

"It is not Bulldog Quarter Horse," said Smith, "and as for how it trots I am not planning to take a beef drive in with it, it is going to be a cutting horse. A really great cutting horse. And it is gonna be broke in the old-time Indian way. Ent it, Ol Antoine?"

Ol Antoine did not reply but Smith did not mind. His ear had scarcely begun to pain yet. He lit his own twisting and blew fragrant blue smoke into the quiet air of the little living-room and he said in an easy voice, "A beautiful thing to see, how an Indian can talk to a horse. He never roughs him up. He never drives the irons into him. He just takes him out, after he gets a halter on him, and he talks to him. He has got just one turn of the halter rope around a snubbin post, like my finger there, and the Indian is on one side of the snubbin post and the horse is on the other side, and he just talks to him. Sometimes he spits in his face a little bit or he puffs his breath up into the horse's nostrils. Like this. *Puh. Puh.* That is the way he goes about it. A beautiful thing to see."

"I never saw any horse broke that way," she said.

"Well, to be honest with you, I am not sure that I ever did. Maybe it was my old dad describing it to me that made it just as clear as if I'd seen it myself. But it is clear in my mind, and I like to have it there, and now Ol Antoine is gonna do it for me in that old-time way, ent it, Ol Antoine?"

Ol Antoine's mouth watered when he smoked and his cigarette was now sodden at the end and would not draw. He dropped it through a hole in the top of the drum stove, but that was the only reply he made.

"His brains have seized up in the cold," said Smith to Norah. "They will thaw after a while and he will remember some of the English language again."

Smith smoked his cigarette until its red coal ate almost into his thumb and forefinger, which had a deep nicotine tan. Norah gave Ol Antoine some coffee, which he took, and a sharp look to which he did not respond.

"Maybe," said Smith, "I ought to get that Shuswap from down below the Fraser to come in talk to that horse for me. You could give me back the ten dollars I already paid you, and I could bring in that Shuswap. Y'know, Norah, them Shuswaps were really good with horses. They had horses before the Chilcotins got them, didn't they,

Ol Antoine?"

"You're wasting your time talking to him on that subject today."

"Also," Smith continued. "I remember that old fellow at Sugar Cane Reserve, he had a great remedy for fixing up frozen ears. An old Intian remety. I don't s'pose you ever heard about what that Shuswap said to do for frozen ears?"

"He did not come up here to talk about horses or frozen ears," said Norah. "Ol Antoine," she said, loudly, "who is in that cabin with you?"

He looked up at her briefly and then down again into his coffee cup.

"Who is there with you?"

"I think you should leave him alone," said Smith.

Norah spoke again, sharply, "Ol Antoine!"

The old man put both hands on his knees and pushed himself up.

"Sit down," said Smith. "We can talk tomorrow about how we get that quarter horse into the corral. Sit down and get warm, Ol Antoine."

The old man walked to the kitchen door. He opened it. A little cloud of steam formed where the warm, moist air of the kitchen mixed with the cold air of the outdoors. Looking back at Smith, Ol Antoine said, "Might be, s'pose you wear a hat, you don't freeze them ears." Then he left.

"You see," she said, "he wouldn't talk to you because I'm here."

"Oh, I don't think he minds you very much. He is really a very tolerant old man, you know."

"Don't always act the fool, Smith. Don't you know who is in that cabin with him?"

"You mean in the love nest?"

"He has got Gabriel Jimmyboy with him, that's who."

Smith's face became still and a screen seemed to be drawn across his eyes, an annoying habit of his.

"Now why would you say that?" he said.

"Because I know, that is why."

"I see. You know."

"Yes. I know. There is no other man in this country would sneak into that cabin the way that man did. No saddle-horse. Just walked in, a couple of hours after Ol Antoine set himself up in there. Smith, that man has never come out of that soddie in daylight ever since the day you buggered off. Sometimes I catch his shadow near that window, but he never comes out."

"Just for seeing somebody come into that old soddie for a visit, I would say you have worked it all up to a pretty good story."

"It is Gabriel, I tell you. I been scared, Smith. Every morning I went out to feed up I put the baby on the wagon with me. I been afraid even to go out to the wood pile."

"Well, why be scared? I mean, even if it is Gabriel. It ain't Gabriel but, even s'pose it is, what is there to be all worked up about? He is not bothering you. Why are you all bothered about him?"

"I am bothered because he is a god-dam crazy murderer, that is why."

"There is no harm in Gabriel Jimmyboy."

"No harm? In Gabriel?"

"Well, he has had his disagreements with the law I know . . ."

"The disagreement was murder, and the police have been looking for him since last October."

"November, wasn't it, I think?"

"Well, all right, November. What difference does it make? He has been hiding out from the police all this time and he is a crazy bloody murderer."

"Well, in a way, but the only time he ever got in trouble with the law was when he was drunk."

"You mean when he shot Haines."

"Yes. He was drunk as fourteen hundred dollars. Had been for months."

"If he was drunk then he can get drunk again."

"Not on this ranch he can't. I should know. The place has has been dry since Cattlemen's Association meeting last October. And Arch MacGregor wouldn't give him any, even s'posin he had the nerve to go down there to the store. And there is no whisky to be had in Graveyard Valley."

"Why did you say Graveyard Valley?"

"Oh, I don't know. I had to say something. It sounded more sensible than Calgary or Seattle."

"I think you know where that murderer has been hanging out. He has been up in Graveyard Valley."

"I never said any such thing."

"Dear God," she said, "how I wish somebody could have put a bullet through that damn murderer months ago."

"Norah, I tell you all is well. For one thing, it will not be Gabriel who is down there. For another, even if it should happen to be him, he is a quiet sort of a man. He wouldn't bother you or anybody else."

"It is Gabriel. I know. And you are going to get him out of there."

"Norah, you are all excited."

"Get him out of there. Because if you don't, I am going to ride down to Arch's store, and get on the telephone, and bring the police in here."

"Now that," he said, "is one thing we do not need on this ranch, is policemen. Quite apart from the fact that you are going to look kind of foolish after they get here, and find it is Macdonald Lasheway or somebody else in the cabin, somebody who is not Gabriel, even apart from that, Norah, I do not feel any need for policemen or any other kind of government people on my ranch."

"Get him off this place," she said, "or I am going to go to Arch's and use the telephone."

"All is well," he said.

"Get him out of here," she said, "or I ride down to get a policeman. Do you hear me . . . ?"

"Oh, all right," he said. "All right, all right, all right all right all right all right. I will go down and tell him to clear out."

He walked to the clothes pegs by the kitchen door and pulled on his coat there, and his overshoes, and as an afterthought he gently fitted a large knitted hat over his small neat head and pulled it down below the points of his ears, remarking, "S'pose I wear a hat, might be I don't freeze them ears."

"No, Smith," she said.

"How's that?"

"No. I didn't mean for you to go down there now, when it's almost dark."

"Exactly when did you figure I should go there?"

"Well, tomorrow, when Ol Antoine comes back. You can tell him that Gabriel has got to go away from this place."

"I see. Or maybe I should send Gabriel a letter, special delivery, registered, air mail. That would be a lot of help, too, considering that he can't read and there is no mail service here."

"Dammit, all I mean is that I didn't ask you to go down there all alone when it's half dark. Don't go down to that soddie, Smith."

"What is all yellow, weighs six hundred pounds and flies through the air?" he asked, and when she didn't offer an answer gave his own: "Two three-hundred-pound canaries."

He snapped the buckles on the overshoes and opened the door to leave.

"Oh, God," she said, "you're so pig-headed. If you got to go, at least take the gun with you. I'll get the carbine from the sitting-room."

"You leave that gun," he said, "right there where it sits. On the wall. There has been enough of this foolishness without people wavin' guns around in the air."

Then he walked out, closing the door firmly behind him, saying, "What has got eighteen slant eyes and catches flies? A Japanese baseball team."

from the novel, *Breaking Smith's Quarter Horse*, by Paul St. Pierre

My Road

There is a length of road a short distance from my home, which I call my road. It runs along between the harbour and the steep rocky forested hill. When I walk this road, as I have ever since I could walk, I have only the water on one side and the high land on the other.

Whenever I walk there, I feel safe and strong and comfortable; a sort of feeling which makes me want to linger there for a while. In winter it is sheltered, and the sun shines on it all day. In summer there is a cool salt breeze off the water.

Where the water is closest to the road, is a sheltered cove, which is never more than mildly stirred by the wind. The water here seems as friendly and peaceful as the thick soft woods and bushes on the other side of my road. The continued rhythm and splash of hundreds of little waves, and the music of the wind in the tallest trees on the hill, make a quiet, changing, but continuous sound which I like to listen for.

Like all other human beings, I have a natural

fear of darkness, but here on my road on the darkest, stormiest night, at any hour, I can walk, and feel no sense of fear. If I hear a noise in the night elsewhere I would immediately picture some awesome beast, but here I have no such impulse. I take it to be a rabbit, or porcupine, or a timid deer, and I call softly to it, until it runs or walks up or along the hill, out of hearing.

Whenever I feel angry or depressed, I walk on my road, throw stones as hard as I can out over the cove or sit in the edge of the bushes or the rocky shore and think things out, and feel better; then I go home.

I believe it gives me more satisfaction and pleasure to walk along this humble stretch of road then it would to tread the Great Wall of China. I think of my road as a friend.

John Vincent Hallett

Boonies

The Night Billy Cooked the Pot

In those early years, we had good tap water in our house, but no toilet. Our boonie was about ninety feet from the house, and it had to be kept immaculate. Pa's strict orders were for us to scrub it daily. The Eaton's sale, winter, or Christmas catalogue was nailed on the left of the seat because Pa was left-handed. He didn't care if we did the splits trying to reach it.

In winter the snow would drift thirteen to fifteen feet high all the way to the boonie, but by some act of God the toilet was clear of snow about three feet all around. After we had shimmied open the frozen door and gone inside, the big weighted pulley would slam the door shut. (In summer months, the sudden impact of this hundred pound stone meant instant death to ants, flies, and snakes that cavorted around the outhouse.)

Once inside we would stand on the seat over the hole as it was just too cold to sit down. We had to listen in case Pa was in the vicinity, as standing over the hole was definitely forbidden, and if he had ever caught us, he probably would have pushed us in. But with the fifteen-foot drifts all along the path, we were pretty safe. With Pa's heavy frame, we could hear him bellow as he sank into the drifts.

Braces were a hindrance at such times. Those miserable little braces, which were always buttoned wrong, would sometimes hold up production until it was becoming really serious. The heavy odorous underwear with the escape hatch in the rear (in case of fire from the sulphur and molasses we'd taken all winter long) had to be cleared for an opening for the posterior.

This was done with sighs and groans, wondering if it was all going to be in vain. Were you going to make it in time? At last your rear would make it through the layers of braces and clothing and with all valves in operation, you'd get that faraway look in your eye as the song "When It's Springtime in the Rockies" floated through your brain. The catalogue with the pages running towards the floor hung firmly on a two-inch spike. We never used the ladies' coats page. It was too colourful—a real pleasure to look at, as though we had company right there with us. At the end of our sitting we would turn to the index where a softer paper was used and where we had from A to Z to choose from.

On the way back you'd find yourself skimming over those huge banks like a mole.

For nightly use, we had small enamelled pots under each bed, which were limited to liquid waste only. This had to be disposed of as soon as we woke up next morning.

One night, Billy, who had been eating laxative foods all day, was immediately summoned. It was bitterly cold and he thought he would take a chance and use the hardware under the bed. Ma and Pa were downstairs playing cards. Just as he was finishing he heard Pa's footsteps on the stairs. Taken by surprise, he grabbed pot and contents and stuck them in the oven of the upstairs cookstove. He streaked into bed and waited for the outcry, but it didn't come. Pa just put some more coal on, stoked the stove for the night, and through habit opened the oven door so that the rooms would get the heat stored up inside. What we got wasn't heat. A gagging noise came from Ma, who at once knew what had happened. Soon the fumes filtered into Pa's room. We heard him leap from bed. He ran through the upstairs, opening every window in the sub-zero weather, trying to entice the foul air to escape. Ma was the type who would speak no more of such an error, but Pa would take it to a judge and jury. This night though because of the fumes he never opened his mouth, and so the sentence had to be postponed until morning. This was a comforting thought to sleep on along with red noses and white ears from the cold.

The Double-Holer

But the old outhouse had seen its day, and its rears. And Pa began building a new one—a double-holer, which around our end of town put us on a level with the elite. We were so excited waiting for it to be constructed that we even held back for two or three days, knowing we'd have company while in progress.

Everything was in pairs to coincide with the double-holer—even two of the latest catalogues, hanging in spots not much farther than the length of your elbow. There were hooked mats on the floor and wallpaper on the walls (which wasn't to be used under any circumstance). Arm rests were nailed on both sides of the openings, which even Henry Ford forgot to put on his first cars. A foot rest on each side was the only mistake, because after you were harnessed into your position, arms under chin and feet on the foot rest, slumbering symptoms took over.

That held up production. We never ever wanted

Pa to catch us in this state, especially two brothers at once, as we knew we'd lose all priority. Why Pa never built a waiting room had me baffled. It's an achy feeling when there are four in a building of this size, two on and two waiting with a hurry up-hurry up attitude on their faces. Sometimes Ted would give you a warning without speaking. Then you knew you had to jump off in a hurry or be sorry for it. Ted's face would get blood red and his breathing would subside; then at the last minute, he'd shiver and we knew we had to get out of the way fast.

This building wasn't partitioned for the sexes, nor did it have a sign to represent the distinction. We were forbidden to attend a session while Ma or our sisters were in conference. Had we known of any union at that time to fight for our rights, we would have gladly consulted it, especially in early autumn with the green apples half-ripened.

Whenever we'd see a brother running like a scalded cat towards the outhouse, we'd automatically accompany him, sit next to him, and swap yarns as though we were on the CPR first class. It had that train effect on us.

Many a head would peek through the curtain if by chance the preacher or a salesman was on his way to the outhouse. We'd peek patiently, hoping he wouldn't mistake the henhouse for the boonie, and try our best to eliminate the thought that one of us should go with him to accompany him on the spare hole.

At times our homework was taken out there. There we'd sit, in dead earnest, long wrinkled pant legs resting on the foot rest. It was a good environment to be in to get away from Pa and study your lessons in peace.

To friends of ours who had one-holers, we four brothers would brag and say very proudly, "We have a two-holer." It was the same as if their father had a Ford and Pa had a Cadillac.

from *Bread and Molasses* by Andy MacDonald

May you have warmth in your igloo, oil in your lamp, and peace in your heart.

Eskimo proverb

Acknowledgements

We are grateful to the following for permission to reprint the copyrighted materials. While we have made every effort to locate copyright holders, we welcome notice of any errors or omissions and will make certain to correct them in future editions.

"In the East Cornera the Pasture", excerpt from W.O. Mitchell, *Who Has Seen the Wind* (Toronto: Macmillan of Canada), 1947.

"Slide Show", "Dumb Indian Failure?", "Who Makes History?", and "Destroying a Nation", quoted by Martin O'Malley, *The Past and Future Land* (Toronto: Peter Martin Associates), 1976.

"A Handful of Earth—to René Lévesque" by permission of Al Purdy.

"Out Along the Prairie", "The Candyman's Cart", Joe Hall, by permission of Eyeball Wine Music—C.A.P.A.C.

"I Want to Get Out", excerpt from Marcel Horne, *Annals of the Fire-breather* (Toronto: Peter Martin Associates), 1973.

"Child's Song", "Train Song", "Honkey Red", Murray McLauchlan, by permission of True North Records, Toronto.

"Where to, Lady?", excerpt from Constance Beresford-Howe, *The Book of Eve* (Toronto: Macmillan of Canada).

"Randying", Ray Guy, *That Far Greater Bay* (Portugal Cove, Newfoundland: Breakwater Books), 1976.

"The Poor We Have With Us Always", Ray Guy, *You May Know Them As Sea Urchins, Ma'am* (Portugal Cove, Newfoundland: Breakwater Books), 1975.

"First Thursday of the Month", Marc Plourde, *The Spark Plug Thief* (Lasalle, Quebec: New Delta), 1976.

"Farewell to the Old School—Again", "Station for a Sentimental Journey", Harry Bruce, *The Short Happy Walks of Max MacPherson* (Toronto: Macmillan of Canada), 1968.

"The Mountain", excerpt from Roch Carrier, *Philibert Is It the Sun,* (Toronto: House of Anansi)

"Youngsters", "The District Nurse", Ted Russell, *Chronicles of Uncle Mose,* (Portugal Cove, Newfoundland: Breakwater Books), 1975.

"The West That Was. . .", "How to Make Your Own Paper", Janis Nostbakken and Jack Humphrey, *The Canadian Inventions Book* (Toronto: Greey de Pencier), 1976.

"Childbirth", Heather Robertson, *Salt of the Earth* (Toronto: James Lorimer and Company), 1974

"Like An Eskimo", "My Little Indian", "Comics House", "Hard Times Killed My Man", "Buying a Human Being", "Hunkies in Town", "Long Before Pearl Harbour", excerpts from Barry Broadfoot, *Ten Lost Years* (Toronto: Doubleday and Company), 1973.

"And The West That Is", excerpt from Heather Robertson, *Grass Roots* (Toronto: James Lorimer and Company), 1973.

"Farmer Needs the Rain", by Roy Forbes, published by Casino Music.

"Secretarial Training '65-'70", by permission of Shirley Miller.

"Some Day", by permission of Dierdre Gallagher.

"Friends Logging", Tom Wayman, by permission of Macmillan of Canada.

"Look What's Become of Me", by permission of Bob Bossin.

"Beau-Belle", Miriam Waddington, *The Price of Gold* (Toronto: Oxford University Press), 1976.

"Street Cleaning", Al Pittman, from Clyde Rose (editor), *Baffles of Wind and Tide* (Portugal Cove, Newfoundland: Breakwater Books), 1974.

"Some Place to Live, My Sons", by permission of Peter Gzowski, from *Peter Gzowski's Book About This Country In The Morning* (Edmonton: Hurtig Publishers), 1974

"Old Alex", "My '48 Pontiac", Al Purdy, *Selected Purdy*, (Toronto: McClelland and Stewart).

"Seymour Inlet Float Camp Domestic Scene" by permission of John Marshall.

"Canadian Railroad Trilogy", Gordon Lightfoot, permission of Warner Brothers Music, Los Angeles.

"Riding the Ocean Limited; or Otto, Spare That Train", and "Our Motto Was, 'Drive 'er Till She Quits, Then Get a Tow Truck'" by permission of Harry Bruce, reprinted from *The Canadian* magazine.

"Ballad of the Red Dumptruck", by permission of Andy Mouland.

"Road Forks and Greasy Spoons", by permission of Matt Cohen, reprinted from *Weekend* magazine, August 7, 1976.

"Silver Wheels", Bruce Cockburn, with permission of True North Records.

"Grease is Cheaper Than Parts", Dave Essig, permission of Peregrin Songs—Woodshed Records Ltd., Emsdale, Ontario.

"The Education of a Class A Mechanic" by permission of Helen Sutherland, reprinted from *This Magazine*.

"Riverdale Lion", John Robert Colombo, by permission of McClelland and Stewart.

"Ten Elephants on Yonge Street", Raymond Souster, *Colour of the Times/Ten Elephants on Young Street* (Toronto: McGraw-Hill Ryerson Ltd.)

"Grandfather and Harry's Trivia", excerpt from Norman Allan, *Lies My Father Told Me* (New York: New American Library), 1976.

"Neighbours", excerpt from Maara Haas, *The Street Where I Live* (Toronto: McGraw-Hill Ryerson Ltd.), 1976.

"Toronto Italian: New World Language", Norman Hartley, by permission of *The Globe and Mail,* Toronto.

"Visible and Invisible in Canada", excerpt from Clark Blaise and Bharati Mukherjee, *Days and Nights in Calcutta* (Toronto: Doubleday and Company, Inc.), 1977.

"On the Bum in Toronto", by permission of Jim Christy, reprinted from *Saturday Night* magazine.

"The Condemned of Kaboni", Angela Ferrante, reprinted by permission of *Maclean's* magazine.

"Potlatch", by permission of Frederic V. Grunfeld, reprinted from *The Beaver.*

"Ol Antoine", excerpt from Paul St. Pierre, *Breaking Smith's Quarter Horse,* (Toronto: McGraw-Hill Ryerson Ltd.)

"My Road", John Vincent Hallett, reprinted by permission of Anderbo Books, Halifax.

"Boonies", excerpt from Andy MacDonald, *Bread and Molasses* (Toronto: Musson Books)

Poem by Takeo Nakano, by permission of the author.

Quotations throughout the text courtesy of John Robert Colombo, *Colombo's Concise Canadian Quotations* (Edmonton: Hurtig Publishers), 1976; and *Colombo's Little Book of Canadian Proverbs, Graffiti, Limericks, and Other Vital Matters* (Edmonton: Hurtig), 1975.

Art direction and design T. Wynne-Jones
Cover by Leoung O'Young
Illustration credits

Michael Solomon 9, 62
Diana McElroy 15, 21, 22, 23
Jerrard Smith 19, 72, 73, 75, 76, 119
Peter McLay 25
Maurice Art Gum 31, 71
Dorothy Duerer 32, 35, 43
Nick Milton 33
R. Stilt-Skeene 34, 46, 48, 49, 50
Zwaantze Jantzen 45
K. Vanderlinden 80, 82
Karen Fletcher 79
Leoung O'Young 105, 114

Photo credits

NASA 7
Leighton McLeod 1, 2, 3, 4, 5, 8, 12, 13, 44, 57, 69, 70, 78, 84, 86, 97, 98, 100, 102
Lenora Hume 10, 11, 37, 39, 125
Vancouver Sun 14
National Film Board, Phototheque
  R.Jaques 47
  Gar Lunney 51
  G. Humter 88
John Taylor 54
Thaddeus Howlonia 58, 59, 60, 61, 64, 65, 66, 67, 103
The Native Press, Yellowknife 107
The National Museum of Canada 108, 110, 128
Martin O'Malley 111, 113
Peter Carver 122, 123
Robert Vander Hilst 91,92,93,95

Notes on the Photographs

p.7 The Earth photographed from a distance of 98,000 nautical miles
p.47 George Merrit, one of the older members of the numerous Merrit
      fishing families; Sandy Cove, Nova Scotia.
p. 107 Richard Nerysoo, himself, 1975.
p. 108 A mass of Coppers, Kwakiutl
p. 110 Bella Coola Indian wearing Echo mask.
p. 128 Face carved in trunk of spruce tree in Northern B.C. said to be
carved by Tlingit to mark northern limit of their territory.

Canadian Cataloguing in Publication Data

Main entry under title:

Earth

(Elements)

ISBN 0-88778-162-4 pa.

1. Readers – 1950–   I. Carver, Peter, 1936–
II. Series.

PE1121.E27   428'.6   C77-001323-6

PETER MARTIN ASSOCIATES LIMITED
280 Bloor Street West, Toronto, Ontario M5S 1W1

United Kingdom: Books Canada, 1 Bedford Road, London N2, England
United States: Books Canada, 33 East Tupper St. Buffalo, N.Y. 14203

To Air From Earth